South Africa
My Vision of the Future

SOUTH AFRICA
My Vision of the Future

Mangosuthu G. Buthelezi

St. Martin's Press
New York

Copyright © Verlag Busse & Seewald GmbH, Herford 1990

All rights reserved. For information, write:
Scholarly and Reference Division,
St. Martin's Press, Inc., 175 Fifth Avenue,
New York, N.Y. 10010

First published in the United States of America in 1990

Printed in Great Britain

ISBN 0-312-05651-6

Library of Congress Cataloging-in-Publication Data applied for

Contents

Foreword	1
1 The powerless liberation struggle in South Africa	7
2 What freedom means to me – my vision of the future	22
3 Business and other realities in South Africa today	37
4 The 'quiet revolution' of Black South Africa	51
5 Black disunity	66
6 Apartheid is in a coma – what will negotiations bring?	83
7 Church and politics – the need for an effective liberation theology	106
8 Sanctions and disinvestment	115
Postscript	130
Negotiations now – who will make or break them?	
Index	149

Foreword

I was asked to write this personal volume to set out my thinking, as it stands at present, on South Africa and its future.

It is not meant to be an in-depth treatise but rather my general views as they have developed in more than four decades as a participant in black political opposition to apartheid.

More than anything I want to convey hope and, conversely, sound warnings of dangers as I see them. I want to say that this black South African really believes that finally the time is near when we will be able to chart a new destiny for this country. My plea is for all those who call this land home, all those who truly care, here and abroad, to start now building bridges of national and international unity and reconciliation.

Our liberty to come must be a universal freedom that is nurtured, loved, respected and enjoyed by all. We must be prepared *now* to work at how we will soon create and maintain good government and continuously exercise the highest ideals of democracy. We must take a hard look at ourselves and at each other.

Much has been written about South Africa and there are many worthy books which offer far broader perspectives than I am attempting at this time. I would not like to be judged on what I have left out. Rather, as I have already indicated, I would prefer that my effort be seen as a highly personal explanation of my thoughts and why I have spent my life working for something tangibly better for all South Africans and, in particular, my black brothers and sisters who have suffered so much for so long.

I have incorporated, in some parts, views that I have specifically and consistently expressed in speeches and in writing over the years. The core of my message now is no different to what I have been saying for many years. South Africa is changing but basic black political attitudes and formal positions have remained constant.

It is my view that both black and white people in this country need to be liberated from apartheid.

I write of my hardships and of those I love who have shared my life, my work and my fears with me. I write of why we came to the conclusions we did at the times we did and why we sometimes stood alone in spite of pressures to adopt other stances. I write of the choices we had and the gut fear in our bellies as we trudged on, hoping against hope that, with all our imperfections, we were playing an honest part in the struggle and faithfully representing all those who looked to us to act on their behalf.

Through all this we were encouraged by a multitude of truly remarkable people who believed in us and supported us with all they had to offer.

Without them we would never have been able to have continued and to have been convinced, as we are today, that we too have something positive to contribute and a constituency to back this up. Politics is, after all, primarily about power and the will of the people to choose their own leaders and promote organisations who present platforms they wish to support.

This book, then, is also a simple tribute to all those who contributed to and shared our vision and determination that non-violence and negotiation were and still are worthy aims and aspirations and who kept the faith in spite of unbelievable pressures.

As I look back I can feel, see and taste the tears of our anguish when, then and even now, all that we have tried to do has been presented by some as being worthless and self-serving or, at best, too moderate for the political palates of the so-called progressive forces. Politicians cry too and there have been bitter heartaches along the way.

I write about the realities around us, the lessons that Africa has taught us over the years, and the kind of future that we believe could offer us genuine peace and prosperity, with human worth paramount in building a society based on all that is universally accepted as decent and compatible with the dignity and rights of all men, women and children.

Today no black South African of my generation could ever conceive of the clock turning back to the time of our youth when, even compared to the evils of racism as they are practised today, we experienced the most appalling deprivation and humiliation because of the colour of our skin.

No black, however humble, stopped striving for decency to prevail in such a way that there was hope for the future.

We all did what we could do and made decisions during times when choices were few and mobility (politically, economically and otherwise) almost non-existent. I accept that I personally will be judged on my decisions and will defend them if need be. We tried, dear God we tried. We walked some very lonely roads and, finally, there is a real chance that in this lifetime our dreams may well be realised.

There will be no overnight Utopia but the black struggle for liberation has always been to gain full inclusion as equals in South Africa and to work alongside others in eradicating racism and ensuring equality of all before the law and equality in a constitution representing the wishes of the majority.

South Africa is finally entering the first phase of transitionary politics towards this goal and now all of us – more than ever before – are on a very perilous path.

The decisions made now will affect governments and generations to come and slowly we are moving forward to meet our fate, whatever it turns out to be.

One of the reasons I have taken the limited time I now have at this juncture to try to encapsulate many of my thoughts in one document, is that I believe it to be crucial that we progress, one positive step at a time, understanding and accepting all that was good and bad in our past while, in a multiplicity of effort, we project what I call a multi-strategy approach and put South Africa first.

This is a call for us to unite as never before; to have trust and faith in each other; to heed the dictates of all our religions because I know of not one that does not prescribe love and respect and reconciliation between all mankind. I want to make the point that I do not believe God has turned His back on South Africa and that He is with us all.

Every South African needs to believe that they can make a difference; that they have a role to play in changing this country for the better.

We now need a multiracial response to a multiracial problem. This should not be seen as a black/white issue (although regrettably it is at the moment) but, rather, a point in our history when the time has come for momentous change.

It is vitally important that the divisions that have been created between us are buried, once and for all, and that blacks and whites come together and recognise that we *all* have a right and a duty to author our new beginning and to equally share in the subsequent construction of our future.

We desperately need debate, dialogue and compassion. There will be no quick fix and if there is, it won't last. We need to formulate long-term positions and strategies that will work here and which will create a national will to succeed. Nobody, myself and Inkatha – the organisation I represent – should be projected as paramount. There is too much at stake.

The obstacles are enormous. It is going to be tough. Our youth are, for the most part, angry and impatient. They want freedom and they want it now. Who can dispute this? It is tragic that many will never really understand the anger and impatience of the generations before them and too often belittle the sacrifices that were made, the virtue in the patience that was displayed, and the circumstances in which decisions were made.

I will write a lot about anger, and about fear, because that is the legacy that apartheid has left us.

I was an angry young man and to this day I am angry at what my family and I have had to endure and the terrible pain we have had to witness. I have had to learn to channel that anger positively and to try to teach that to others.

We have watched a once prosperous and respected country all but crippled financially and the mere mention of its name become an international signal for derision. Worst of all we have seen lives destroyed and families torn apart, not only by government action but by the fierce will of people to oppose apartheid as they saw fit.

It has been a unique civil war all of its own and both black and white have experienced families and communities bitterly divided. We have all buried our dead and lived with our heartache – and our prejudices.

There is not a South African who hasn't been touched by apartheid in some way or another but the black majority has been humiliated beyond belief by it. We are now snarling at each other, killing each other. At the same time we have seen ever-increasing numbers of well-intentioned anti-apartheid activists. In their own minds they have skilfully taken sides on issues to further the cause of peaceful co-existence. In reality they have proceeded to further exacerbate tensions by highlighting divisions instead of consolidating black and white opposition to all that is hateful and wrong.

There are many forces at play and numerous agendas and yet, miraculously, I have no doubt that the vast majority of black South Africans still put the achievement of reconciliation through negotiation as the country's highest priority. There is now evidence that ever-increasing numbers of white South Africans want this too.

The revolutionaries abroad, many of whom have waged an unsuccessful armed struggle for more than twenty five years, are also angry and impatient. Their dream of returning as a government from exile is slowly but surely fading away as national imperatives take hold within the country. Any role they will play will be according to what they have to constructively offer a post-apartheid South Africa. Their scenarios for the future will be scrutinised along with all the other political options which will one day be placed on a negotiating table.

The time is ripe for democracy to emerge on South Africa's political centre stage. We also run the risk of the country falling prey to strategies that will fail; of ruthless manoeuvring that will be the downfall of us all.

Nobody can predict the future, least of all I. Our destiny is uncertain as the momentum for change intensifies and the country is faced with varying political, social and economic options. In the end, the people will decide and I have great faith in the people of South Africa.

White extremists and black extremists are being shunted into the obscurity they deserve and what better sign can there be?

I am in awe of the men, women and children of black South Africa who have, step-by-step, in a veritable tidal wave of determination and necessity, broken down the barriers of apartheid. The victory to come will be significantly theirs and deservedly so because, for the most part, they have met their objectives with dignity and without the kind of hideous violence (advocated by some) which would truly have torn the country asunder.

They should be an inspiration for *all* the people of South Africa and an international example of how the poorest of the poor can resolutely overcome injustice without having to indulge in despair and destruction.

The authors of apartheid and their successors and supporters are staring failure in the face. You can smell the rotting carcase of this vile and evil legislation throughout the country, from Cape Town to Pretoria, from Boksburg to Carletonville.

Now we have to come to terms with our past and prepare for the future while acknowledging that although many have had the strength to withstand the assault that apartheid has had on the souls of so many, others have been grievously wounded.

I think that in many ways there was an element of forgiveness and compromise inherent in the political rationales of previous generations of black (and white) activists that is rapidly becoming extinct within the breasts of today's young radicals. Some have already lost these precious human qualities.

In setting out my thoughts and feelings, again and again the subject of the unity of the nation became paramount. It is for this reason that I have, for the most part, deliberately avoided attempts to score points against and highlight individuals and organisations which have declared themselves my adversaries for one reason or another and to dredge up the rights and wrongs of our unhappy past associations, whatever they may have been or continue to be. I have had to make various observations regarding some but I have attempted to make them in the context that nobody should be excluded from being involved in authoring a new South Africa. If I am criticised for this, so be it. The time has come for us to bury our differences as much as we can and I would not like this book to be used as yet another launching pad for bitter recriminations and retaliatory unconstructive argument.

It is enough for me to say that the nature of human experience since time began has been about diversity of opinion and the right of all men and women to freely express themselves as they see fit. South Africa needs all voices to be heard and my point of view is a part of this whole.

If I have one particular prayer it is that the once revered spirit of African humanism – Ubuntu/Botho – experiences a rebirth throughout this continent in order that there be true reconciliation between all and that we learn to love and to share with fervour and to agree to disagree with intelligence and humility. There has been too much hate, too much distrust, too much betrayal. It has tainted us all and it is time we moved on.

The powerless liberation struggle in South Africa

Since wars begin in the minds of men, it is in the minds of men that the defences of peace must be constructed – *UNESCO Constitution*.

The above quote came to mind when I was thinking of where to begin to describe the multiplicity of efforts directed towards change in South Africa and the obstacles we are facing. This is a book by a black South African primarily about black attitudes, as I perceive them, and in so doing my first function must be to acknowledge and give credit to my fellow South Africans who have more than proved that they are capable of contributing towards the establishment of a future worth having. They have been overwhelmingly unswerving in their commitment to basic democratic principles.

This statement may appear to be contradictory when I describe, as I will, the role of pro-violence revolutionaries in our midst but these are people who are, quite clearly, marching against the expectations of the vast majority of South Africans. Their views are also contrary to the conclusions drawn by the founding fathers of the African National Congress who founded the organisation in 1912 to oppose racism and segregation by employing the tactics of non-violence and negotiation.

It is also important not to sideline the sacrifices and supreme efforts made over many years by large numbers of white South Africans and others internationally who have been no lesser foes of apartheid than we have and whose dreams are our dreams. When the final chapter in the struggle for the liberation of this country as a whole is written, they too must equally share in the glory of our overall triumph. However, their invaluable contribution has been such that it deserves to be the subject of a book on its own and I cannot now adequately credit the immense role they have played. I must state for the record that any essay or study on the struggle against racism, segregation and apartheid has to acknowledge their role.

It is my contention that the majority of black minds in South Africa have *always* been set on achieving victory over the racism we have been forced to endure in such a way that ours will, above all, be a consummate, unparalleled, and dignified conquest of the worst of colonialism and all that it has spawned. Dignity, in African terminology, has very special connotations and I use this word frequently because it means so much to us. Dignity in this sense is best encapsulated in the ideal of Ubuntu-Botho. It is humanism in its all-embracing sense.

There is something very deep-rooted about the central values in the black struggle for liberation in South Africa and they can be traced to the great personalities among the founders of the ANC which was subsequently banned by the Government in the 1960s.

They were the true South Africans who dreamt of a multi-racial democracy and who mounted non-violent tactics and strategies which would make the achievement of a multi-party, multi-racial democracy resting on a one-man-one-vote system of government a reality. Throughout the country there are countless individuals and organisations who are determined that these ideals will be realised and I am one of them. The national liberation organisation, Inkatha, of which I am President, is another. This is why I have stated again and again that Inkatha, founded by me in 1975, is structured in these ideals as propounded by the founding fathers of the ANC in 1912.

Some now say that democratic opposition to apartheid has failed. Democracy cannot fail. Only those who abandon democracy fail. Democracy as evolved throughout the history of mankind has never been achieved in one fell swoop or one stroke. It has been a slow process.

For us in this country there is no prospect of any lasting democracy unless there is a multi-racial, multi-party democracy. A one-party state in South Africa would be a prescription for an ongoing series of revolutions and counter-revolutions.

Nowhere across the whole of Africa is there any country in which it is as imperative as it now is in South Africa to accommodate the political aspirations of every race group in a political system which is reconciliatory. Conciliation will be the true harbinger of peace and security in the hearts and minds of all South Africans and more than anybody else, generations of blacks throughout the country have already shown that, although the victims of a multitude of racist sins and revolutionary fervour, it is they who first held out the olive branch in seeking an undivided country and it is they who have held it aloft for so long in attempting to build a new South Africa.

When I meet ordinary black South Africans going about their daily lives, at work and in their homes, I am always struck by the dignity with which they conduct themselves and this is why I say that our victory can be a dignified one.

Some of our numbers, I realise, have anger and hatred in their hearts and retribution on their lips, but I am talking about the black masses as I know them who, often in the midst of the most wretched conditions, have learned to live with a smile and with a caring for others that swells me with pride for them.

The extraordinary humanity of black South Africans will, I truly believe, show the world that against all odds black and white can live together and build together and that this quality will awaken those whites in whom history and circumstance have created a false sense of supremacy, a new sense of love and respect for all fellow men.

This is not a pipe dream. I know it won't come overnight but it can happen and that is all that counts. With my experiences of life I am not naive about human failings but as a Christian I can never not believe that God's message of reconciliation is not possible. Nor do I for a moment imagine God is dead.

I often tell theologians and others who come to meet me that I do not believe that every human being in South Africa is pushed beyond the realms of being able to enact Christian love. I do not believe that this country has yet to be punished by God to the extent that He has turned His back on us and leaves us to kill each other. I believe He demands our reconciliation one to the other. Reconciliation after all involves not only reconciliation between man and man but also between God and man. Even with political equality, which we will achieve, the overall situation won't improve until the battle against poverty, ignorance and disease has finally been successfully accomplished and, as I have always stressed, equality of endeavour can receive equality of reward.

There is a political battle for hearts and minds being waged at present and a war of many dimensions has been under way for a considerable time and yet it seems to me that, whatever our turmoil, ordinary blacks have been aware that peaceful, construc-tive stances and actions are paramount. Why else would millions of black South Africans have stomached what they have done and, on the whole, rejected wholesale and organised violence against their oppressors – and within their own ranks – if they had not innately believed in this?

Non-violence and negotiation is what the *real* black struggle for liberation is all about and it is, I think, appropriate to start this book with what is surely in the hearts and minds of the majority of South Africans. They know that, as unjust and as evil as apartheid is, above all they must reach out for something worthwhile, something decent that history itself will recognise as a triumph of human endeavour at a critical juncture in our turbulent times.

Instinctively the majority of black South Africans have, over the decades, sought democratic processes to achieve what is rightfully theirs in the land of their birth. They have looked to the courts; they have organised peacefully and been torn apart in the process; their leaders have been imprisoned and detained without access to the law; they have petitioned and prayed; they have marched and been shot; all this and more.

When white suppression seemed insurmountable, terror of another kind began to proliferate and there are historical reasons for this. In short, more than two decades ago, some of our numbers in exile gave up on non-violent tactics and strategies and, with considerable backing from various quarters, launched an unsuccessful armed struggle from abroad and attempted to create a people's war within the country. I have said time and again that I understand why some blacks have grown disillusioned and have lost heart. I understand how apartheid has pushed them beyond human endurance and they have abandoned things of great value. However, the consequences of their disillusionment have been catastrophic in terms of pain and suffering, black unity, and multi-racial reconciliation.

I do not believe that the pro-violence stance taken by certain groups in exile necessarily reflects the views of all in exile. To a very large extent they have become the victims of their isolation abroad and have been out-manoeuvred, for the time being at least, by those representing certain countries and political organisations and ideologies who wish South Africa to emerge as a one-party state espousing Communist/Marxist/Socialist principles.

Many who now hold leadership positions in exile, as I knew them in the past, were not Communists. They were black South African Nationalists. This dichotomy, now, within their own ranks has yet to be properly addressed and resolved by them for their own reasons; cohesion and financial support and aid being important factors. However, as our liberation draws closer and having been tackled, as we are trying to do, peacefully and democratically within the country, there is every reason to postulate that those abroad will face serious internal traumas in the not too distant future.

In some ways this is why the political battle in South Africa (and internationally) has shifted quite considerably towards a struggle to author what kind of post-apartheid society we will have, now that this evil system is all but dead on its feet.

Forces are broadly ranged now between those who want a multi-party free enterprise democracy in a federal-type unitary state and those who are determined to create a one-party socialist-type unitary state. Other minority interests and mostly racial and sectarian options form other categories.

So now we are entering into a battle of another kind and the forces of darkness, the forces of iron ideological will and determination are still with us. For some there will be no compromises while in reality, compromises will eventually have to be made by all and they will be made.

Those who have turned to guns, limpet mines and bombs show no sign, at present, of a change of heart. Blacks and whites continue to be horrifically maimed or blown to pieces in city centres, supermarkets, restaurants, at bus stops and on farm roads, ostensibly in the name of a minority who think that they will be able to make South Africa ungovernable by creating turmoil and in preparation for seizing power – terminology that they themselves have used in their propaganda. Statistics released by the police and printed in the Press show a tenfold increase in attacks on state and civilian targets over the four years up to the middle of 1989, (*Citizen*, May 2, 1989).

In addition, quite separate from the force used by the State to maintain the status quo, there is also right-wing white terrorism within South Africa whose agents support various bigoted minorities of would-be demagogues who are attempting to gain power of another lethal kind. They, however, present marginal dangers to our long-term security and the fascism they represent can and should be outlawed now and in a future democratic government.

Political manipulation, factionalism and fanaticism has been thrust onto innocent communities throughout South Africa and

11

freedom of political choice made a life and death issue for many. Blacks are dying, whites are being assassinated and all in barbaric and intolerable circumstances. The stakes are now very, very high because real black/white negotiation is within our grasp. White power is fragmented to a very real degree and democratic political accommodation has become an economic and social imperative.

There can never be a return to classical Verwoerdian apartheid and finally the indications are that there is a growing body of individuals and organisations nationwide who can be drawn together to take part in a new movement towards solving the South African problem through non-violent means.

Ultimately, political power will be awarded to those who are truly relevant to the needs of blacks because South Africa is one country and the majority are black; it is not a country of minorities. Political power is power that moves with history and not against it. That power must be relevant to the majority but relevant in such a way that *all* are beneficiaries of that power regardless of race, creed or any other determinant.

Radicals are under pressure especially, precisely because they quite correctly perceive change coming in such a way that they may not be among the major players.

The history of Southern Africa is turning to underwrite the importance of non-violent power bases. It is the politics of negotiation which will finally win and in my discussions with various leaders of the Western world, all totally concur with me on this point.

Throughout the world where revolutionaries have been active they go about their revolutionary business to establish revolutionary governments. Revolutionaries are not beneficiaries of non-revolutionary forces. They do not conduct revolutions so that others can set up governments. There are revolutionaries in South Africa and in exile who now feel threatened because there are increased prospects of peace through non-violent means. They do not want victory brought about through the politics of negotiation. They want to be victorious in order to set up their own revolutionary government and to return from exile as the *de facto* and *de jure* rulers of the land.

The process through which change will finally come about must be one in which the minority who are opposed to a multi-party democracy achieved through non-violent means are out-manoeuvred so that it is they who, in the end, must sue for peace.

There will be no revolution and power will not be seized by the people in South Africa. No organisation will return from abroad as a government from exile. There is absolutely no doubt about this. Power is going to be negotiated by those who have real power bases and well defined and realistic political, social and economic positions acceptable to the majority of South Africans.

This is why I would like to urge all those in exile to come home and join this political process and not attempt to undermine it. Their voice is needed too. A new South Africa is going to emerge from a process in which diverse groups will have participated. I want my brothers and sisters in exile to be a part of this process.

Negotiations are going to be conducted between those who have demonstrable constituencies and who have consolidated their supporters and received acceptance of their platforms at grass roots, throughout the country. It is only a matter of time. We have to accept that there will be no Lancaster House-type conference –as there was regarding Zimbabwe – in which to settle the South African situation. There will be no overnight moves into a new constitution. There will only be a process in which gains are made sporadically as skirmishes are won and imperatives drive more and more South Africans into the same camp.

The South African government has never been weaker than it is now if one measures weakness and strength by its ability to maintain apartheid. We all know that apartheid is totally impossible to maintain. It must be destroyed; it will be eradicated.

Black South Africa is on the march and nothing will stop it. We are seeking what is legitimately ours and there is nothing that the South African Government can do to stop us.

There is now, historically speaking, less reason than there has ever been before to resort to violence to solve the country's problems. There is every reason for all those in exile who believe in democratic processes to lay down their arms and to be with us when the final, fatal, blow against apartheid is delivered. An unequivocal renunciation of violence would be their passport home and we would welcome them with open arms and hearts. I can't think of a country in the free world that would not put substantial pressure on the South African Government (in addition to our own voices from within) to insist that they be allowed to return and to openly organise and consult with their supporters here.

The struggle has been an integral part of our lives for so long and no matter if individuals and organisations continue to differ over political and other tactics and strategies now and in the future, we all have a right to lawfully put those tactics and strategies to the people in such a way that citizens are free to accept or reject them. I would not have it any other way and I would never be a party to the future of this country being authored by certain groups if others were excluded.

The reality is that unless those in exile who currently support the armed struggle are persuaded to participate peacefully in the final thrust towards establishing a democratic South Africa it is they who, as I have said, will have to sue for peace to this end. Events will overtake them.

We have entered an era of flux and change and we can now expect that more and more groups will have to break away from positions they have firmly held in the past. This will have consequences which will not always make for plain sailing. As each group faces the necessity of abandoning positions or changing postures, it will have to overcome the internal tensions this will involve.

Nevertheless, organisations declared by the United Nations and elsewhere as the sole and authentic representatives of the black struggle for liberation and their surrogates – aided and abetted primarily by certain church leaders, various academics, political figures and some sections of the media within the country and abroad – continue to somehow live and operate in a political Disneyland. They attempt to create an aura that it is they who will ultimately author the guidelines for future government; it is they who will direct change.

Real change can only come from within South Africa and from the broad base of the will of the people, no matter the leaders and organisations to which they subscribe. The people are the sole and authentic voice of liberation in this country. South Africans, here on the ground, must author the future.

I will always subscribe to what has been described as a bottom-up approach in constitutional affairs and anti-apartheid tactics and strategies. A top-down approach, whereby a dominant clique decides on constitutional reforms and anti-apartheid action on behalf of the people, is manifestly undemocratic.

Ignoring these realities, some organisations and their surrogates pursue tactics and strategies which the masses have rejected. Sanctions and disinvestment are a typical example of tactics that have gone wrong. Some consciously, others, to be generous, unconsciously, have been a part of the creation of a climate of fanaticism in which blacks have been expected to accept their dictates without question. Those who have not bent to their will have been eliminated by extremist forces or have faced assassination attempts and political and media ostracism. I am one of the latter. Should they not have a democratic choice? Should I not have a choice?

All sides have been caught up in the conflict resulting from this intolerance of opposition and quest for ultimate power and such has been the action and counter-action that none can now claim that elements within their organisations are blameless for the overall carnage that has resulted. What started off as a classic campaign to unilaterally capture the political loyalty and fervour for freedom of the populace, has hideously backfired.

Unless revolutionaries turn to assist in doing what needs to be done to raise democratic opposition to apartheid, they will become locked into an upward spiral of violence in which neither they nor their adversaries will emerge as winners. I refuse to walk the road of violence because it is a losing road. Along it one will not find victories of the kind that our heroes and martyrs in the black South African struggle for liberation dreamed of.

Intimidation, political and otherwise, has been rife in various forms; families have lived in endless fear and while some have endured with the stoicism of saints, others have vigorously exercised their right to self defence and freedom of political choice – and worse.

In the process many young men, women and, equally tragically, children have been drawn into killing fields of mindless retribution and a type of gangland warfare that only poverty, ignorance and deprivation can produce. Our society has yet to come to grips with the problem of how to care for them now that many are isolated from their families and communities and, without doubt, deeply emotionally damaged.

So, having not attempted to gloss over the fact that, yes, blacks are killing blacks, whites are killing blacks, blacks are killing whites, my point is that we are not dealing with a situation in which this is mass action. Television coverage and media reporting may well present a scene of a country on the verge of blowing sky high with pent-up tensions on the boil, but this is quite frankly not the case.

The *de facto* National Party Government is having to rule under a State of Emergency but the machinations for change are on another track altogether because the country is functioning and the State is intact.

Furthermore, hard on the heels of the white backlash to this somewhat minimal threat to security (given that South Africa remains the strongest government, militarily speaking, on the continent of Africa) has come a black backlash. Within their own communities and in the more responsible black Press, the word is out that anarchistic behaviour is unacceptable.

In the onward march of history revolutionaries were thrown up as one black response to apartheid but more importantly history has thrown up other black responses. Blacks are sick to death with being bullied, not only by whites but equally by their own people. It is un-African and the more articulate in affected areas have finally found the courage to stand up and be counted.

The power of words, tough talk and a cohesive message that they will no longer tolerate the shame of this blot on black pride and dignity has been enough in some quarters. I salute them.

Other conflicts have yet to be resolved but God, willing, they will because I return to my premise that ordinary black South Africans have shown, time and again, by their individual and mass actions, that they eschew behaviour and strategies which will impair their dignity and the dignity of others.

Revolutionaries and counter-productive influences attempting to militate against an evolutionary and non-violent process towards the democratisation of this country are phenomena which we are simply going to have to deal with along the way as best we can.

Apartheid is the real problem, apartheid has been the root cause of the majority of our ills and whether we like to or not we will have to deal with its effects for a long time to come.

How blacks generally have dealt with apartheid is another matter altogether. They have, for the most part, employed personal and result-orientated tactics and have gone about achieving their aims and aspirations with dogged and quiet determination. I refer to the way that blacks have stealthfully penetrated previously white social and economic domains and have made sure they are there to stay.

Laws had to be changed not because of magnanimous actions on the part of white legislators but because blacks had created a situation in which they could no longer be enforced.

Job reservation, pass laws, influx control, separate amenities in some areas and the Mixed Marriages Act are classic examples. It is only a matter of time before other hated and obstructive Acts of Parliament are also rescinded.

In a kind of silent revolution blacks within South Africa have steadfastly marched forward towards their ultimate destiny determined to survive whatever demeaning and inhuman treatment was forced upon them.

Along the way some have lashed out, conflicts have been won and lost and the dead have been buried honourably and dishonourably. There have been moments in this period of our history, as I have described, when all blacks have been shamed by the excesses exhibited by some ostensibly on behalf of all.

The surge of international revulsion towards apartheid has given us hope and inspiration while, regrettably, it has also created divisions between us. We needed the condemnation of the Western democratic world against an abhorrent system, but, for many in the forefront of that condemnation, existed opportunities for personal and collective political gain in their own countries and in the process sides were taken, leaders acclaimed no matter their constituencies, monies allocated for sectional gain, and venomous propaganda disseminated which has been disastrously harmful to the very people they purported to be assisting. Black unity has suffered as a consequence.

This is not to say that international revulsion towards racism accompanied by aid and political muscle has not been welcomed by us and sincerely acknowledged as inordinately helpful and desperately needed in a myriad of ways.

However, the fact still remains that the divisive polemic some politicians, theologians, influential foreign correspondents and others have proclaimed as the truth, has played a part in rupturing the black body politic and only black South Africans will be able to heal these wounds. The battle for a new beginning for justice and equality will ultimately be fought and won by us in our country.

Black and white South Africans who share our dreams will damn apartheid to the hell it deserves and establish a country in which there is equality of opportunity and equality of reward no matter an individual's race, colour or creed. We desperately need the Western world to applaud these goals, encourage us along the way and support us when it can, but in such a way that it is recognised that *we* must be our own liberators and *we* must choose our own leaders. When you really think about it, isn't it somewhat racist,

17

somewhat demeaning as far as we are concerned, for people to assume that black and white South Africans seeking democracy are incapable of orchestrating their own liberation?

For me it is the ordinary people of South Africa who are the salt of the earth. It is they whom God has created in His own image. It is in them that the real sovereignty of South Africa resides. It is the ordinary people, the ordinary man and woman, the ordinary child, for whom politics should strive and for whom political leaders and others should direct events. I have often said that it is in the ordinary people that the ultimate wisdom of how to live together must be found and that is why I continue to place such emphasis on this. It is the good of the ordinary people and only the good of ordinary people which counts.

In every black township, in every rural homestead and in every ghetto there is an awareness of the realities of South Africa today and what is required for the future. Black families are pulling together as never before. Education has become an imperative even though some foolishly advocate 'liberation before education' and schools and books are burned in the name of the cause. What cause damns children to a lifetime of illiteracy? And yet, it boggles the mind that this very slogan was taken seriously and reported nationally and internationally as a sign of serious and effective black revolt.

These veritable babes in arms are led to believe, to this day in some areas, that they are going to bring down the Government. Schools have been targeted as the stamping grounds for revolutionary propaganda and although this is also not a new phenomenon throughout the world, various journalists and broadcasters have conveyed this as somehow being an integral part of the struggle here.

Mercifully the very people who advocated this crime against children appear to be back-tracking on this strategy (the concern of parents has been considerable) and it is worth noting that more often than not it seems to be the case that those who shout the loudest about the bravery of a new breed of young people with iron in their souls, those who are in the forefront of this vacuous revolutionary tactic, are the ones whose own children are, or have been, safely sheltered in private schools within the country or abroad. As with sanctions, the ones who seem to live and eat in the best manner are the ones who advocate a stringent diet and humble accommodation for others!

Attempts to turn children into anarchists disgust me and no matter what our deep and very real grievances, it is my belief that our children are a gift from God who should be protected and nurtured. Those who orchestrate this heinous behaviour have yet to answer for their crimes; not so much in a legal sense but morally because, as a result of their agitprop, tens of thousands, perhaps millions, of black youths have unwittingly forfeited, or will very soon forfeit, the only real chance they have of making a better life for themselves. Time will march on and they will be left behind. Schools are lying in ruins, good teachers have fled the profession. Millions will be unemployed because already there are too few jobs and the under-educated will certainly be last in the queue.

The fires that these snakes in our pockets attempted to kindle within our youth have, to a large extent, died down. Triumphantly, black South Africans have continued to fill every school and strain every educational institution to breaking point in their demand for education for their children. That is a reality.

When I write about black determination to succeed, I must show, as I am trying to do, that blacks have been prepared to suffer, and watching parents suffer as I have done to educate their children, is proof enough to me that human endeavour has emerged victorious.

In South Africa brothers and sisters contribute towards educating their siblings. There is a vast unselfishness about black South Africans when it comes to education that has always inspired me to have an even deeper faith in human beings than I have ever had before.

It is because education is so fundamentally important and because commitments to education run as deep as they do in black South Africa, that I am always so totally appalled when party political hacks and amateurs in human decency – nationally and internationally – drag whatever education there is to offer in this country through the mud and use it as though it were a latrine where filthy graffiti can be written on walls. I tell parents, teachers and school inspectors that I am incensed by those who enter a school premises with anything other than awe for what is going on there, however humble it may be and whatever the limitations.

Education gives freedom, education gives the minds of men and women in today's world the capabilities to construct the defences of peace. When people ask me what they can do to help my people I always invariably reply: 'Educate them.'

Survival has been our ultimate imperative and when I see children walking long miles along country roads through the dawn to attend a village classroom while their mothers are already tilling fields, I know that the will to succeed is there. Pictures in my mind of urban commuters crammed into segregated and overcrowded trains and buses as they head to work tell me the will to succeed is there. The smiling faces of black university graduates, so-called socialites, businessmen and other entrepreneurs beaming from the pages of magazines and newspapers tell me the will to succeed is there.

Black South Africans can see the road ahead, they can walk the rough and the smooth, but they know where they are going.

Apartheid is dying because of these people. It simply had no hope of succeeding when so many, each in their own way, set out to destroy it. History itself deemed it a freak and social and economic realities have finally sounded its death-knell.

I believe that we have reached, to some extent, a no-holds barred point in South African history. The only thing that matters now is to mount something that will now work. I would not, however, regard any solution as having worked if it replaced one kind of tyranny with another kind of tyranny in South Africa. I would only regard a solution as having worked if, in the end, it gained democratic freedom for all the people in South Africa and left a government of the future in a position to govern, after its political victory, in such a way that the battle against poverty, ignorance and disease could proceed with real hopes of success.

That is why I do not intend to make extensive ideological statements or party-political statements on behalf of Inkatha or the KwaZulu Government, of which I am Chief Minister. Anything that could work, done by whoever did it, would benefit me and all the people I represent and care for. We will back anything that will really work. By the same token, we will resist anything that may immediately work in the short term to finally destroy apartheid but will involve South Africa paying crippling prices in the future.

Politics and diplomacy must ultimately be rooted in reality. In both politics and diplomacy I have often said it is a fact that ideals are mixed up with subjective judgments. These serve to dramatise truth and guide actions but ultimately political representations which distort realities put the parties concerned beyond the ability to deal with the realities they talk about. I call for action that can work because it is action that does not try to ignore having to deal with realities.

Black politics is not divided into liberation forces and the rest who work to maintain the status quo or profit from it. There is a vastness about black politics in which the major forces of history are at work. It is these forces which will bring about a new South Africa and it will be a new South Africa that arises as blacks and whites salvage the best that there is and jettison the worst.

What freedom means to me – **2**
my vision of the future

I know not what course others may take; but as for me, give
me liberty or give me death.

Patrick Henry, 1736–1799

Of what use is political liberty to those who have no bread? It
is of value only to ambitious theorists and politicians.

Jean-Paul Marat, 1743–1793

Whenever we take away the liberties of those whom we hate
we are opening the way to loss of liberty for those we love.

Wendell L. Willkie, 1892–1944

*L*iberty is a precious possession of which there has been little in
abundance for black South Africans. Liberty can be defined; you
can see it, you can feel it in those countries whose citizens truly
enjoy it.

Liberty means many things and as we approach the glorious day
of the liberation of South Africa from the evils of our past, my first
thought is a wish that our new-found freedom will be a lasting
freedom and that our fledgling liberation will be one in which the
majority will have participated freely and fairly. That they will
have made choices free from anger and recriminations; free from
prejudice and fear; free from intimidation and coercion.

Only a negotiated settlement will give us this; wars give the
spoils to the victors and those who gain power through the barrels
of guns usually rule through the barrels of guns.

Our liberation must not be a fleeting thing. It must not be, for
some, a gateway for their pursuit of naked political power, rigid

ideologies, revenge and corrupt personal gain. Privileged cliques must not emerge overnight and become a new breed of ruthless and disgraceful exploiters backed up by position and power. People's fears must not come true.

For the ordinary man and woman liberty should at last mean the chance to stand tall and to be free to live and to work as equals in the land of their birth. Those whom they choose to govern them must cherish this and listen to the people. They must be honest and open; they must not promise the impossible. They can offer dreams, they can offer hope and inspiration, but all must be grounded in reality and the people must be made aware of these realities.

For me, the liberty of South Africa will hopefully mean that we will all have a chance, at last, to reach out to each other with open hearts and on equal terms and to constructively build human resources and all the other resources of the nation. All this and more.

My vision of the future for South Africa is simply one of unqualified growth in human, spiritual, political and economic terms. Constitutional and political reforms must be of the people and for the people.

I cannot be prescriptive, I cannot detail explicit and exacting political formulae at this stage. I am adamant that the people must decide and that individuals and organisations must be free to put their choices to the people. Inkatha will be one of them and our membership, which numbers 1.7 million now, will formulate positions and platforms which will be tested among the people for their acceptability. We have already come to certain conclusions which I will enumerate later.

There will be no liberty and the struggle for our liberation will have been worthless if the freedom we seek now is not a freedom that can be made to work for all in the future. That is where we in Inkatha are coming from. I have always said that following free and fair elections I would serve, if requested, any democratically elected government and its leadership and should we be placed, in the same way, in positions of power, I would hope that others would, likewise, work with us.

I do not clamour for the highest office in the land. My fight for black liberation and a united, non-racial and democratic South Africa is a struggle for all South Africans. I am doing what I believe to be right in the circumstances which now prevail.

My vision is of an all-embracing government of the future which will cut across all barriers; a government which will have what the Americans so beautifully call checks and balances.

No government in a post-apartheid South Africa should be placed in a position where it can abuse this gift of liberty; where it can, through mismanagement and uncompromising ideological dogma, create a situation in which growing and grinding poverty destroys the foundations upon which we must build. Poverty is the enemy of democracy; poverty is more often than not a recipe for revolution. Desperate people do desperate things.

I was asked, many years ago, the ten things I would do if I were in a position of power in South Africa. I answered, as I have said, that I do not seek political supremacy for my own sake, but the thoughts I put down then are, on reflection, the same today.

Quite naturally, I could not have replied as I did if the hypothetical government of the future of which I was supposedly a part was not democratically elected and based on a nationally acceptable constitution and a Bill of Rights which would entrench and protect the rule of law.

These are fundamental and non-negotiable conditions for me. I wrote then, that:

(1) My first priority in a post-apartheid government would be to attempt to reconcile and unite all South Africans and bury apartheid's bitter legacy of division and despair. I would exhort all South Africans to open their hearts and their minds and to build a lasting national spirit of caring for each other and sharing a common love for our land. I would invite all those who have left our shores to return and work with us in creating a new order in which decency and democracy are the cornerstones.

(2) I would set about gathering able men and women around me from throughout the country who would share the responsibility and privilege of governing South Africa in such a way that their every action would be aimed at establishing equality of opportunity for all. I believe that a post-apartheid South Africa will need leaders capable of reaching out and into every facet of life in this country and understanding and determining the needs of our people and then acting effectively. This government, to have any lasting utility, would have to consult the people and avoid the politics of prescription.

(3) An inherent part of the formation of the Government would be a new constitution and a Bill of Rights already accepted by South Africa as a whole. It would be the duty of the Government to immediately ensure that all the provisions contained therein were upheld and to this end I would look to our Courts and our learned Judges to inform and instruct the Government in each and every area where decisions and action should be taken to protect and realise the inalienable and equal rights of all citizens.

(4) I would appeal to commerce, industry and to workers to interface and cooperate with the government in critically examining our economy and determining what should be done in the short term and long term to launch a veritable explosion of growth and job opportunities. A stable and buoyant economy will be vital for our future stability as a nation and this would be a priority. The free-enterprise system must be proved to be just that – free and enterprising, not only for the rich but for the underprivileged attempting to enter the system. I would underscore time and again that I agree with the maxim that the best welfare system is a job. Trade unions must be supported and encouraged by the government and, in responsibly fulfilling their obligations to their members, be given information and access at all times to decision-making which will, in the final analysis, engender trust and a healthy interaction between employers and employees at all levels. The aged and infirm must be loved and protected and the State must be in a financial situation to do so. We must care in practical and efficient ways and not just say what we'd like to do if we had the money. In many ways the measure of any society is the manner in which it provides for those of its citizens who are unable to do so themselves. The survival of the fittest should not be the national name of the game in a new South Africa.

(5) As a part of the national effort to stimulate our economy I would look abroad for international aid and expertise and would welcome genuine and constructive offers of assistance from all over the world. I see South Africa as being an integral part of a multipolar world.

(6) Diplomatic and trade links should be re-established throughout the world and we should seek entry into political, scientific, cultural, economic, academic and other worldwide organisations and institutions while opening our own doors to exchanges of this kind.

(7) I would look especially to the rest of Africa and seek friendship and unity of purpose in a variety of areas. I would offer South Africa's assistance in working with these countries (to our mutual benefit) wherever possible and would go, perhaps, even further if necessary in proving our bona fides by attempting to give what we can in the true spirit of pan-Africanism. In doing so my goal would not only be to promote peace and harmony throughout Africa but to attempt to set in motion the economic recovery of the region as a whole. There is no doubt that South Africa's input could be of inestimable value in this regard.

(8) Leaders must move among the people and in so doing I would set about encouraging our universities and other educational institutions, religious and cultural bodies to pursue and to reach greater heights of excellence in all they do and to stimulate the nation to debate, share and participate as never before on a myriad of levels. This nurturing of the mind and spirit goes hand in hand with the actual physical health and welfare of all people and if we are to develop a society in which there is hope for generations to come, then every facet of the needs of men, women and children must be explored and taken cognisance of.

(9) In honouring the rule of law, a representative government in a multi-party, free-enterprise, democratic South Africa must see that all that we cherish is rightfully defended and to this end our police and our defence force must be of the people and for the people and, without fail, reflect the will of the people in all that they do. At the same time, civil servants have an equal responsibility to give of their best. I would therefore appeal to men and women of calibre and commitment to come forward and serve their country with wisdom and distinction and, in turn, be properly rewarded for their efforts.

(10) Finally, there are few nations who can truly be called great that do not exhibit to the world a sense of dignity, compassion, a capacity for humour and an ability to look on the bright side and overcome whatever comes their way with honesty and common sense. I would encourage these attributes because I want to see a happy South Africa in which people are proud of their country and their achievements, individually and collectively. It is not going to be easy. We have a hard and a long road ahead of us, but unless we are all prepared to give it a go, what hope have we?

This is the vision I aspire to and always have; these are the basic ideals and thoughts I would like all who support me to share with me and to work alongside me, and many others, in achieving.

Utopian fancy? I think not. What I have written is not unique. I think these are merely words that encapsulate the feelings and desires of the majority of South Africans. There are, of course, other groups who represent obvious ideological exceptions and who are committed to their own agendas for South Africa for their own reasons.

Within them lie many of the causes for fear, for suspicion, and this fear was succinctly outlined by a newspaper editor, Ken Owen of *Business Day* in Johannesburg, in a column on May 8, 1989, headlined 'It's what happens after liberation that worries them.' He wrote: 'Change in South Africa is certain: the survival of democracy, even of tolerably civilised existence, is not. The abolition of apartheid is half-accomplished, and the reforms have unleashed forces which will undo the rest of it; the uncertainty, the source of our insecurities, is what happens then?'

He said, and I am only quoting a small portion of the article: 'Liberals know that the alternative to apartheid lies not in transferring power, nor even in sharing power, but in taming it. The key to a solution of the South African problem is to entrench and protect the rights of the individual, and to weaken the State. It is to make every man's home his castle, a place of safety.

'The techniques to achieve this end are well known elsewhere, if unfamiliar in S.A. which has never been a democracy. To tame power it is necessary to disperse it as widely as possible. Among the ways to do so is the division of power between competing branches of government, so that each balances the other; or the division of power between regions, so that each will protect its people against the central authority . . .

'Self-evidently, individual liberty cannot exist without private property, and a lawful means to transfer title. These two concepts lie at the heart of economic success wherever it has occurred. S.A., like the Soviet Union, is failing in part because it has violated both concepts.

'Ownership of property has become an uncertain thing, so white voters fear – and many black people expect – that liberation will see them stripped of their possessions and their security . . . (two) economic spokesmen (for political parties) deride the idea that black people can be persuaded of the superior merit of free-enterprise capitalism . . .

'They have lost faith in, or perhaps they never believed in, the liberal idea that the poor can be turned into wealth creators if they are set free . . .

'White voters are terrified of what will happen when power passes into black hands, but nobody – neither black nor white – tells them how they may live safely under black rule. White voters think they will be impoverished by liberation, but nobody tells them that the economic growth that has enriched others can enrich this nation too . . .

'What the anti-apartheid white electorate needs – is almost begging for – is a vision of a tolerable future.

'That vision cannot come from socialists, obsessed as they are with class vengeance and with bureaucratic control; it cannot come from the nationalists, obsessed as they are with balancing groups against each other; and it cannot come from the neo-conservatives whose extreme economic libertarianism lets the devil take the hindmost.

'Only the liberals have a credible vision of a secure future, if only they could convey it to the electorate in terms which the voters find credible.

'Instead the voters are subjected to a steady stream of threats, warnings, denunciations and moralising sermons that serve to heighten their anxiety . . .'

When I read this I had already been asked, more than a year before, to write of my vision for South Africa and this book was already well under way. However, Ken Owen's articulation of white fear struck a chord in me, because I have also written about this over the years at length.

I recognise that there is white fear. I understand it. There is black fear too, which I know only too well. I recognise that some whites arrogantly cannot perceive that black South Africans will actually support the free-enterprise capitalist system with its history of exploitation. Little do they understand that in many ways black South Africans have been fortunate that this country is the last on the continent of Africa to be liberated.

We have been able to heed the lessons that Africa has taught us. Socialism, as it has been practised, hasn't worked on this continent. With the best will in the world in some countries, it has failed miserably. The fact is that the free-enterprise system remains the only system in which wealth can be generated in such a way as to provide the jobs and infrastructure necessary for growth and stability.

I don't need to elaborate on the reality that from the Soviet Union to Zimbabwe, the merits of free enterprise are becoming all too apparent.

The destruction of Western standards and capital bases is the last thing whites should fear in South Africa. The black struggle is about inclusion in this system of the creation and enjoyment of wealth. They want to be a part of the best that there is in this country.

The notion that black South Africans are future looters and plunderers of white possessions is equally insulting. While the fact remains that whites have ransacked Africa for their own gain for centuries and that in South Africa whites control 87 per cent of the land, an hysterical picture of blacks turning the tables on whites is preposterous if democratic principles finally emerge triumphant. South Africa is not yet a democracy and that is the crux of the issue. Will it become one, and how, is the question on many lips.

Obviously there will have to be a future redistribution of wealth in South Africa but this does not imply overnight wholesale dislocation for the haves in favour of the have-nots. Radicals and others may well send shivers down the spines of many when they talk of nationalisation and Africa for Africans but doesn't this get back to the reality of what kind of government a post-apartheid South Africa elects?

If the people opt for a socialist one-party state, of course there will be dangers aplenty. I don't think they will. I think there is every indication that the broad mass of people genuinely want a multi-party, free-enterprise democracy and I keep reiterating this over and over again. Numerous well-documented surveys support this view. Isn't it high time, then, that all South Africans and those internationally who wish to see this become a reality, started working towards this goal now?

Whatever the overall desires of the people are, good politics is always about the reaffirmation of established and accepted aims and aspirations. People need to be continually convinced that they were right in having made the choices they have and these choices must always be open to debate and consultation. The majority must be comfortable with these choices; they must know that they are not alone in their convictions.

We must accept that others who do not share this particular objective of a multi-party, free-enterprise democracy, are going to continue to pursue their own aims and in so doing attempt to win over support to their cause. Hardline ideologues are more often than not highly motivated and extremely articulate. They have access to the media and they exploit their advantages with breathtaking commitment and often with a ruthless disregard of the so-called rules of fair play.

They are out there batting to win. Is this not a democratic right? Whether they would, in other circumstances, likewise extend this magnanimous and democratic attitude towards freedom of political association to their opponents is another matter altogether. Nevertheless, under no circumstances should we debase this right and deny it to others however inconvenient it may well be and however threatened we may feel.

Why is it that they can seemingly appear more organised, more determined? Why is it that their voice is more often than not the loudest?

Quite simply because the rest of us need to get our act together.

All those who desperately desire freedom, a multi-party democracy and the free-enterprise system to emerge as a reality in South Africa must get out among the people and sell it. There must be ceaseless campaigns across the length and breadth of the country and our opponents must, quite simply, be outwitted and outnumbered by sheer strength of purpose and conviction. Blacks and whites must work together to achieve this. If we don't then won't we deserve what we get?

Frightened whites must not sit back and, as Ken Owen noted in his *Business Day* article, 'wait for Armageddon, quietly polishing their rifles in the sun, as somebody put it.' His was an appeal, as I understood it, primarily for whites to galvanise themselves into action and to support the liberal vision of a secure future. I'm sure he meant blacks too, who share similar values.

We do face some very sombre scenarios in this country. If we paint a picture of the future based on the assumption that the South African Government will remain recalcitrant in the eyes of the international community and tenacious in following its apartheid policies in the eyes of South Africans, we must necessarily paint pictures in which violence is on the ascendancy and will remain spiralling upwards until scorched earth policy meets scorched earth policy.

If we paint pictures of a future based on the assumption that the South African Government will in the end put deed to word in bringing about the kind of reforms that the majority of the people in this country will regard as truly meaningful, then we must paint a picture of a period of turbulence through which we must walk. Negotiations will only become negotiations when there is a defined objective ahead.

The era of political prescription in which whites could dictate to blacks is passed. South Africa is one country, there must be one citizenship for one nation. That must be the objective.

Negotiations in our circumstances mean playing risk games. Every sane and sensible political leader wants to minimise risk but we can only minimise the risk inherent in real negotiations to a certain point. Beyond this point, the risks we avoid incur far greater risks in the development of the country's revolutionary climate.

One thing I am quite sure of is that time favours revolutionaries. The more time that passes, the more revolutionaries gather their strength and the more support grows for them in society at large. We cannot get on with the job of tackling poverty, ignorance and disease until we have developed a national will to do so and make a united national effort to succeed. While poverty, ignorance and disease spread rampantly in black South Africa, the fertility of revolutionary seed-beds increases.

We do not have the time to teeter on the brink of taking real action on the level of negotiation. We must stop milling about at the cross-roads of history and move forward to meet our fate.

I am one of those who agree that Government action is pivotal for success in the politics of negotiation. We cannot negotiate a new South Africa into existence without the South African Government and the National Party being party to the negotiations. I am one of those who believe that the politics of negotiation must salvage the best that there is and jettison the worst in order to get continuity and progress towards a really democratic South Africa.

Continuity will be assisted and the ability to safeguard the best there is will be enhanced if the future is governed into existence. All-or-nothing demands of total capitulation and the handing over of power by the South African Government are a recipe for a devastating war in which there will be no winners.

The South African Government is a *de facto* and *de jure* government. It is childish to jump up and down and call it an illegitimate government. I have not heard one person describe military juntas, which we have in such abundance in Africa, as illegitimate once they become *de facto* and *de jure* governments of their particular countries.

The government in South Africa today is wrong; it is not representative; it is not democratic, but it is the government of the day and it is a government of the day which must be salvaged from the consequences of its own actions.

Democracy alone can ensure the survival of democratic ideals. Democratic ideals cannot be preserved by dictators or fascist governments. They cannot be preserved if they are kept in some kind of political suspension while the South African Government rules by power derived from a perpetual state of national emergency. Political ideals can only ultimately be preserved in exercising them.

There is no place in South Africa for people who believe in decency and democracy yet sway this way and that with the passing winds; or who bury their heads when the going gets tough or run away to what they think will be safer climes.

I am not in the habit of shaking when somebody confronts me politically and I will not be intimidated out of deep commitments to things that are really worthwhile. White South Africa need not fear sharing the country with black democrats.

The issue of fear raised by the Editor of *Business Day* is fear which I acknowledge as being a prime factor in the South African political equation but not only is there fear in white society but there is fear in black society too.

I recognise how difficult it is going to be to banish fear and, in the meantime, how terribly damaging it is to the process of negotiation in South Africa.

Whites are afraid of any kind of majority rule. This is not surprising because racism produces fear of other race groups. It is based on that fear. There is fear in black society that as long as whites are given any kind of special treatment, they will use their position to perpetuate apartheid.

There is fear that whites cannot in fact abandon their racism. In the whole of South Africa revolutionaries in fact represent only a minority of all the people. It is, however, a minority that has been growing and in this minority the fear of the future is so dominant that only the complete destruction of apartheid, together with the destruction of multi-party democracy and the capitalist free-enterprise system, is regarded as sufficient to ensure that white racism is broken forever.

We face the realities in South Africa that if the degeneration of the political situation continues, we will end up with fear producing a situation in which, as I have already stressed, none will be the victors. We must move away from this eventuality and we must therefore deal with fear.

Blacks will continue to fear any moves whites make while the South African Government continues to cripple black democracy by banning and imprisoning leaders and restricting organisations. With the total leadership of black South Africa free and working for the future, we as a country will be able to develop the democratic process in which democratic activity is welcomed and encouraged.

It is white fear of black democracy that leads to the curtailment of black democracy. In turn, it is the curtailment of democracy that leads to fear of perpetual white domination.

This fear on both sides must be taken seriously and one of the ways we can do this is to compromise. We must cut down on the preconditions we insist be met before we negotiate the future of South Africa. Black South Africans must recognise that prospects of a one-man-one-vote system of government in a unitary state which rests on universal adult franchise really does strike fear into white hearts.

White South Africans must recognise that prospects of any kind of apartheid or neo-apartheid, or any kind of constitutional dispensation resting on racist cornerstones, strikes fear into black hearts.

I personally cherish the ideals of a one-man-one-vote system of government in a unitary state. All of my adult life I have hoped for a Westminster-type parliamentary system in South Africa. The vast majority of black South Africans cherish such a system of government. We must, however, put South Africa first and be prepared to look at a federal system, a canton system, or any other kind of system in which the fundamental principles of democracy as expressed in the constitutions of the free world are preserved.

I express the view that South Africa cannot rediscover the wheels of democracy. We need to recognise that there is a free world and that a democracy which serves the free world could serve South Africa.

There is in South Africa a rising groundswell demand for the normalisation of the country as a modern, Western-type industrial democracy. To speed up the repeal of apartheid is synonymous with calming racial fears and gaining acceptance for the ideals of

Western industrial-type democracies resting on the free-enterprise system.

Four years ago I put forward an example of the kind of Declaration of Intent needed before meaningful talks about power-sharing and reconciliation could commence between the S.A. Government and others. I did so because I believed whites were misled about what black South Africa wants. I made it clear then, as I do now, that we do not demand to dominate as blacks over whites. We seek only to share in a way in which whites can join in. I said then, and I repeat now, that if we cannot do this, then what is there to do?

My draft declared the following:

We declare our commitment to serve God in obedience to His divine will for our country and together recognise that:

☐ The history of mankind shows the need for adaptive change among all peoples and all nations.

☐ Nations which have managed to avoid the use of violence in the achievement of national objectives are the nations which have grown in wisdom.

☐ Both mistakes and lessons not yet learned led to errors of judgment in the mainstream politics in both the black and white sections of our society.

☐ The South African people are a family of mankind, seeking to live in harmony in the African community of nations and seeking to do so by expressing civilised ideals in the practical, social, economic and political affairs of our country.

☐ The South African constitution as it is now written is by force of history and reality a first step in constitutional reform which urgently needs the second step to be taken of enriching the constitution to make it as acceptable to the broad mass of African opinion as it has been acceptable to the broad mass of white opinion.

☐ The Westminster model of government was not ordained by God to be the only form of good government.

We therefore accept that:

☐ The need to make the preamble to the South African constitution of equal value to all the groups and peoples of the country by enriching the clause 'to respect, to further and to protect the self-determination of population groups and people' to include the notion that this can best be done by sharing power. We need to share power in such a way that no one can dictate to any other group how to express its own self-determination, and we also need to share power in a formula within which the hallowed values of good government are not compromised.

☐ The need to preserve the constitutionality of the adaptive democratic process on which we will jointly rely in being subservient to the divine will for our country. We will therefore together seek:

☐ To negotiate as leaders to amend the South African constitution to make it more acceptable to all groups.

☐ To find an alternative political system to that which the world at large understands by the word 'apartheid' and also to seek an alternative political system in which universal adult suffrage is expressed in constitutional terms acceptable to all the peoples of South Africa.

☐ To give expression to the common citizenship of all South Africa's peoples without qualifying the meaning of citizenship for any group.

☐ To use the opportunities presented in practical politics at first, second and third tier levels of government to fashion national unity by deepening the democratic process, and to use the democratic process in exploration of what needs to be done to get the people to legitimise the instruments of government.

We therefore pledge ourselves:

☐ To express national pride and patriotism by insisting that South Africans will decide South Africa's future in the acceptance of each other as individuals and groups and the acceptance of each other's cultural rights to be who they are.

☐ To start where we find ourselves in history and to move from there to build on all that is positive and valuable and to change that which is negative and undesirable.

☐ Each to work in our own constituencies to develop a South African pride in managing our own South African affairs in harmony with internationally accepted standards of civilised decency without being dictated to from without.

Having thus declared, we stand together to defend our right even with our lives to take the steps and the time needed to establish consensus between groups and to win support for our joint efforts in the South African family of nations.

Furthermore, to stand together to defend South Africa from external onslaughts and to stand together to resist any use of violence which threatens the politics of negotiation aimed at national reconciliation.

As a black South African I drafted these words for all South Africans to share with me and debate. These words were totally supported by my constituency in KwaZulu and Inkatha. They were rejected by the white leadership of the South African Government.

They were a vision then of how we could get the politics of negotiation off the ground. My intention was to join blacks and whites together in a determined effort to move purposefully into a new future.

This was a black initiative and one which I believe is even more relevant today. Whites must not fear blacks. Blacks must not fear whites. What more can black South Africans like myself do but continue to say this and to attempt to prove our bona fides over and over again?

Business and other realities in South Africa today

3

The object of government in peace and in war is not the glory
of rulers or of races, but the happiness of the common man.
Sir William Beveridge, 1879–1963

The three ends which a statesman ought to propose to
himself in the government of a nation, are: 1. Security to
possessors, 2. Facility to acquirers; and 3. Hope to all.
S. T. Coleridge, 1772–1834

A baby is born every 26 seconds in South Africa. Eight out of 10
farm workers cannot read or write. By the year 2000 there will be 13
million black children at school. An estimated eight million people
could be unemployed by the turn of the century. The cost of
housing could be as much as R50,000 million over the next 12 years.

These were the chilling statistics I read in a newspaper (*The Star*,
May 2, 1989) quoting the S.A. Directorate of Population Development.

According to the Government's Central Statistical Service (CSS)
the estimated South African population (excluding the so-called
'independent' homelands) at the end of June 1987 was as follows:

African	20,132,000
Asian	913,000
Coloured	3,069,000
White	4,911,000
Total:	29,025,000

The 'independent' (Transkei, Bophuthatswana, Ciskei, Venda – TBCV) homelands account for a further 6,181,898.

In its Race Relations Survey for 1987/1988 the South African Institute of Race Relations noted that the total South African population may be estimated as follows:

African:	26,313,898	including a small number of white, Indian and coloured people who have been included in this figure because they live in the 'independent' TBCV areas.
Asian:	913,000	
Coloured:	3,069,000	
White:	4,911,000	
Total:	35,206,898	

Revised figures for the number of births for Africans in 1985 and 1986 were not available. However, the Institute quoted research attributed to the President's Council saying that the African population's fertility rate was currently five children per woman. This means that today, realistically, South Africa has a black birth rate of approximately three per cent.

The chief executive of the Association of Chambers of Commerce and Industry of South Africa, Mr Raymond Parsons, was quoted then as saying that South Africa's high population growth would have a 'paralysing effect' on the economy's capacity for growth, job creation and raising standards of living.

The Department of National Health and Population Development, in its annual report for 1986, noted that the South African population growth was one of the most urgent problems facing the country. The report said that there was a clear link between rapid population growth and poverty, unemployment and poor socio-economic conditions. A balance should be struck between population growth, basic resources and 'economic and social capacities.' Population growth could be contained only by improving the quality of life of the fast-growing sectors of the population through social and economic development programmes and family planning.

These are the realities of South Africa today and in the future. History has taught us that political, social and economic fundamentals are irrevocably tied together.

The production of wealth is going to be vital for the stability of any government and I have already made it clear that I believe that only the free-enterprise system could possibly build on what is positive in South Africa. We, and I am referring to black and white South Africans, do not want a situation to develop here which mirrors what we now observe in Mozambique and Angola and other parts of Africa.

We have the distinct advantage now of witnessing a whole Southern Africa in which there is a general reaching out for free enterprise to bring salvation to poverty-stricken countries.

Mozambique, which tried so hard to walk the socialist road, is once again turning to the involvement of free-enterprise business in the development of the country. The Soviet Union is wanting to withdraw from regional conflict in Southern Africa and now, more than ever before, South Africa is the Western world's gateway to Southern Africa and a great deal of Africa beyond.

I see it as imperative that we open these gates wider and that we handle our own internal South African affairs so that what happens here becomes beneficial to the rest of Southern Africa. What use would we be to the rest of Southern Africa if we added to the poverty on the sub-continent by botching the process of bringing about change?

In everything we do we must look at South Africa's location in Africa. South Africa is not an island unto itself and we will be destroyed by a southern sweep of revolutionary tendencies coming out of poverty-stricken Africa if we do not go on the offensive and spread development far beyond our borders.

As it is in South Africa, time is running short. Millions already only barely exist on charity and associated development or feeding schemes. Poverty, ignorance and disease are rampant. Parents must have homes and jobs, children must be fed, clothed and educated. Employment must be created for the huge population bulge that is about to enter the market place. Figures today show that fifty per cent of all black South Africans are under fifteen years of age. The twenty-first century is, in some ways, already upon us.

When I think about South Africa's economy I know that we must start generating wealth to a far greater degree and we must start now. We can't talk about the wholesale redistribution, in a post-apartheid government, of what we already have; we must start planning jobs for the future, homes for the future, schools, technikons and universities for the future, clinics and hospitals for the future. The needs are endless.

My own political and economic approach to the questions we

face in South Africa is one in which I attempt to look at the realities as a sober pragmatist and not as an ideologue. I am in the business of politics to lead because the people need leadership; I am not in politics to satisfy my own personal requirements. I therefore have the advantage of being able to stand somewhat aside from the in-vogue thinking of the day and I do not have to conform and please audiences simply because I want to be acceptable. I have to constantly look at tomorrow and to avoid doing today what will not last until tomorrow.

The enormity of the problems stare me in the face every day of my life. I know that there are already millions of black South Africans who are pouring from poverty-stricken rural areas to the cities in search of jobs and are living in vast spreading slums and squatter areas. I know that there is no prospect whatsoever of eliminating the horrendously high unemployment rate in South Africa in the foreseeable future, even under optimal economic growth rates.

This is why I look closely at and recognise the vital importance of the survival activity in the informal sector of the economy, as blacks create many forms of cottage industries.

I have been particularly interested, in this regard, in the seminal study published by Hernando de Soto, author of *The Other Path: The Informal Revolution* (Harper and Row) on the critical role being played by the informal sector in Third World economies.

This powerful and convincing study of conditions among the poor in Peru reveals striking similarities to the South African situation. In describing the process in which the poor and homeless in Peru 'invade' and settle land, in precisely the manner South African squatters are doing, de Soto observed that these new arrivals reject, utterly, the 'socialist' assumptions that demand collective ownership of property and immediately set about dividing their newly acquired land into private lots. They establish their own systems of law to protect each other's private title to that land. This point has been especially highlighted by reviewers of the book in South Africa.

De Soto says the rural poor in Peru who come to the cities fight to get a foothold in the system (South Africa again) but that they are fighting to get into it, to join it, not to overthrow it (South Africa again).

This is the reason, he argues, why socialist schemes in Latin America have failed, especially in view of the fact that liberal governments tend to alternate with fascist military regimes.

40

De Soto observes that poverty exists because the poor are prevented from creating their own wealth and are particularly hampered by laws and regulations 'the burden of legal affairs in enterprise in Peru' and a lack of access to the law (South Africa again). In Peru the informal sector began to generate its own body of laws which 'we have seen at other times and in other places in the world . . .'

In an article published by the Centre for Strategic and International Studies in Washington and in the *S.A. Foundation Review*, de Soto postulated: 'The informal sector may yet emerge as the new middle class, as its predecessors did in Europe and North America. It is fair to say the informals share common interests and objectives . . .'

De Soto notes, and I totally agree with him: 'The only real solution is for governments to do what the people best require. People are much wiser and smarter than they are generally given credit for . . . Our conviction that democracy and market economies are the only path to development grows out of a pragmatic test of what works and historical perspectives that offer substantial supportive evidence.'

He echoes my thinking precisely when he states that many of the conventional wisdoms about the way modern economies emerge are simply irrelevant to circumstances in the developing world 'and we have much homework to do to put our intellectual house in order.' It was too simple to conclude, as many did, that by sweeping away all bad legislation matters would improve.

Nobody in the West had drawn a blueprint of 'how to traverse from the mercantilist system to one based on a market economy and an open political framework . . . we must do the ideological work of putting together a body of ideas and policies that hang together convincingly and embody human aspirations and our moral preferences . . .

'The advent of Marxism-Leninism means that we cannot trust in the leisurely drift of history as the West would, to stumble on a modern political economy. The simple answers posed by this philosophy have a certain power appeal, especially among politically active élites . . . It is ironic indeed that a system that has produced such oppressively dismal economic results throughout the world has nevertheless taken over half the world's governments.'

De Soto argues that not only the Marxist-Leninists should be 'deliberate' in their ideological approach and that the importance of change in basic socio-political affairs is a subject that should not be left to them alone. 'It has been their province, but we must lay claim to it,' he quite correctly urges and cogently adds:

'We can also be deliberate by studying the history of the developed world to understand how deregulation, administrative simplification and good macro-economic policy can be translated in the reality of the developing countries so as to produce a language that the majority – a group the developed world knows little about – will support.

'Economically prosperous and politically liberal systems are not beyond the reach of the developing world. People who want real answers instead of dogma must understand the forces at work and address their recommendations to those powerful and emerging actors in the developing world whose efforts are the cornerstone of a better future . . .'

All his research suggested the 'central importance of effective democratic governance to the prosperous functioning of an economy. If our concept of democracy is limited simply to periodic electoral exercises, then our concept is too narrow to meet the demands of economic wellbeing . . .'

I have taken the liberty of quoting Hernando de Soto at length because this is the type of thinking that South Africa desperately needs. We must draw on experiences and realistic analysis such as his which give hope and inspiration.

We are still in a nightmare situation where blacks in this country are being battered economically and politically. Laws, as in Peru, baffle and inhibit would-be black entrepreneurs and stifle initiative.

As if the going wasn't tough enough internally, international economic political sanctions have added to our despair. They have hit black South Africans and they have hit us hard. The downturn in the economy (linked primarily of course to Government policies) has created all-round insecurity. White expertise and money is fleeing the country; international corporate responsibility to black South Africans is rapidly diminishing as company after company pulls out. The value of our currency on international markets has become a joke.

When I study the implications and effects of sanctions the only conclusion that I can draw is that they will, without doubt, slow down the pace at which the balance of economic power can shift in favour of blacks.

I am extremely angry about the cruel manner in which certain South Africans and pro-sanctions lobbies abroad dictate what is good for black South Africans and arrogantly assume that we are prepared to suffer.

I argue that punitive economic sanctions are measures the West feels it can take as one of the few, or the only, option available to it to express its disgust of apartheid. But these are Western perceptions giving rise to Western reasoning which we as black South Africans reject. I appreciate the outrage Westerners feel when they see how blacks suffer under apartheid and I appreciate their humanitarian concerns and moral statements. I question whether they have the slightest understanding of the political agendas of certain individuals and organisations within South Africa and abroad who urge them to do what they are so blindly doing.

I have a growing concern that Western democracy and Western concepts of justice and equality are concepts which many in the West apply to themselves in their own home circumstances with meticulous care, but apply to us here in South Africa with a great deal less care. By imposing sanctions they are dictating to us and I would not use that word if this was what we wanted.

This is why it is so tragic that friends of the South African struggle for liberation so disregard the well-documented views and sentiments of the majority of blacks who are the victims of apartheid, which I will detail in a later chapter. Blacks reject sanctions and disinvestment because they know that an economy cannot be turned off and on like a tap. They know that jobs lost will be lost forever.

A recently retired veteran anti-apartheid and human rights campaigner, Mrs Helen Suzman, the longest-serving Parliamentary Opposition politician in South Africa, expressed in an article in the *Washington Post*: 'It is surely senseless to blunt the only weapon with which blacks can improve their position at the work place and beyond the work place.'

My colleague, Dr Oscar Dhlomo, the Secretary-General of Inkatha and KwaZulu's Minister of Education and Culture, put his perspective of sanctions in another way: 'Apparently the rationale is that instead of breeding chaos, violence, repression, economic depression, black unemployment and poverty, sanctions will bring order, peace, democracy, economic growth and liberation. Black people, however, want to be liberated on their feet and not as corpses and unemployed mendicants.'

Unemployment figures continue to soar and blacks struggle to survive. Cape Town University's deputy vice-chancellor and social ethics professor, James Leatt, noted in a speech in 1988 to delegates at a Black Management Forum congress, that South Africa faces 'catastrophic unemployment' and that the country's demographics are 'ticking away like a time-bomb.'

Professor Leatt says that between 33 and 44 per cent of South Africa's economically active workforce (the majority being black) cannot be accommodated in the formal sector of the economy on current development trends and economic growth indicators. He estimates half of the eligible work-force in South Africa is likely to be jobless by the year 2000 if employment is not created, which ties in with figures mentioned earlier from the Directorate of Population Development.

He stresses a fact that is little appreciated. There is a 'powerful fiction' abroad that South Africa is a relatively wealthy country whose problem is that its wealth is in the wrong hands. 'Irrespective of who owns the wealth of South Africa, this is a comparatively poor country with a GNP per capita eight times lower than the United States and four times lower than New Zealand,' he says.

South Africa, he added, is a developing country grappling with the twin challenges of industrialisation and democratisation. There is 'considerable comparative evidence' that market-related industrial development is the most powerful engine of wealth generation the world has known. As Adam Smith observed, there is an organic link between commerce and liberty.

It is clear that those of us who take figures produced by academics such as Professor Leatt seriously, those of us who have to live among the poorest of the poor, simply have to get on with the job now of encouraging growth and stimulating job creation in the formal and informal sectors. We have to heed the advice and accumulated experiences of the Hernando de Sotos of this world who have witnessed how free-enterprise and democratic principles can work hand in hand.

We desperately need the West to assist us in the economic development of South Africa and it must assist in the vertical mobility of blacks in South African society. We need more investment; we need more markets abroad; we need more training schemes; we need more education and we need more community development schemes.

Investment capital brings with it management skills and new

technologies and perhaps just as important as anything else, new markets. No developing country still saddled with the problems of millions of people living in a Third World subsistence economy can make any real progress without substantial injections of foreign investment and the ability to trade its wares effectively nationally and internationally.

Countries in the West, by invoking sanctions and disinvestment, are hampering genuine economic and political development in South Africa. They should take a hard look at the whole of Southern Africa and see the extent to which prospects of democracy have fled before advancing poverty south of the Sahara.

The forces that can be generated by foreign investment should give rise to diplomatic and material support for the best that there is in opposition to apartheid. Countries who enjoy the benefits of the free-enterprise system should not have double standards and insofar as South Africa is concerned express their abhorrence of apartheid by supporting whose who are opposed to the free-enterprise system. It doesn't make any sense to me but that is, in fact, what is happening.

I reiterate that when I talk about the huge deficits in South Africa, particularly with regard to the black majority, I am talking about things that cannot be fixed overnight and this must be clearly understood by all. We do not have the capital or enough artisans and other professionals to build the houses, hospitals, clinics and schools that are needed. We do not have enough teachers to educate the rising millions. We do not have enough doctors.

Whether we are talking about teaching, or nursing or skilled artisans, the time that we will consume gathering together those that can be taught and teaching them, will be time in which the population bulge increases yet again to exacerbate every problem we are attempting to solve.

The backlogs are enormous and the following available figures also tell their own story:

Once again, according to the Department of National Health and Population Development, if the country's present birthrate is maintained the following may happen: South Africa will have a population of 47 million in the year 2020. Presently, South Africa's population doubles every 34 years and 56 out of every 100 people are still illiterate.

Illiteracy among South African women is nothing short of horrific: many millions cannot read or write.

If South Africa is to reach parity by the year 2000 with regard to expenditure on education for the various race groups, it will need to spend 18 per cent of its GDP as opposed to the just over four per cent presently being spent.

For this to happen the South African economy will have to grow by seven per cent per annum. With the impact of sanctions and disinvestment, the economy was expected to grow by only two per cent in 1989.

The South African Government is already admitting defeat. The government's ten-year plan to equalise education standards between black and white by the year 1996 is 'unattainable', according to the (then) Minister of National Education, Mr F. W. de Klerk. The country's growth 'had not generated enough funds to allow for the necessary increases in spending . . . Although progress has been made, sanctions and disinvestment, with other factors, contributed to the plan not being realised.' (SAIRR, *Social and Economic Update* 30 April, 1989).

Latest statistics available (1986) show that average black earnings were 27.5 per cent lower than white earnings.

The South African Institute of Race Relations reported in a recent publication, *Social and Economic Update*, that some 1.8 million people live in 'informal' (squatter) settlements around Durban. In the Pretoria/Witwatersrand/Vereeniging area the estimated back-log for housing is between 350,000 and 370,000 units.

It added: 'Some 71 per cent of Africans need a subsidy to afford any housing at all, according to the latest figures released by the National Building Research Institute . . . which also finds that 45 per cent of the total African population cannot afford to make any contribution to housing – they need a 100 per cent subsidy . . .

'Almost half of the African population still cannot afford any contribution towards housing given current transport and food costs. These calculations are based on the disposable income of Africans, rather than earnings . . .'

According to various reports, while 4,000 new black managers will be required annually until the turn of the century, only an average of about 300 black people have, at any one time, been occupying executive positions in established corporations in South Africa.

While black consumers buy 54 per cent of the groceries purchased in South Africa annually, formal black retailers account for only 4 per cent of retail grocery turnover.

I am always amazed when international visitors from the First World visit South Africa, with its First World urban facade covering Third World realities, and talk in terms of First World standards becoming a reality for the majority here once apartheid goes.

The First World exists in the kind of luxury the Third World can now not even aspire to. There are no prospects of creating an African continent in which the per capita consumption of raw materials and of energy approaches anything like the consumption in Western Europe and North America.

We face the fact that there is just not enough raw material for the whole of mankind to live the affluent lives of the West European and North American.

The facts I face present me with very stark choices. I will do anything and everything that should and could be done to alleviate the suffering of my people. I know with a deep horror just how much really desperate poverty in many areas produces appalling infant mortality rates. I know how malnutrition diseases spread and how diseases like kwashiorkor, pellagra and tuberculosis are rife in many areas. I know of countless areas where dysentery spreads because there is no sanitation, insufficient safe water and not even minimal standards of hygiene.

Everything that can be done must be done to ease the suffering of the poorest of the poor. Therefore I cannot indulge in ideological niceties. I must be a pragmatist.

It is the realities around me which scream out that we dare not reduce in any way prospects of creating employment and of generating the wealth that any government of the future would need to begin tackling the poverty problem in South Africa. All political history teaches me that ideologies do not survive when they do not result in people actually perceiving that they are better off.

No government in a future South Africa will survive unless the people feel that their lives have been improved because of it. Any government which destroys prospects of job creation, and destroys prospects of increasing personal income, is a government which will be thrown out by revolution. Any revolutionary government which takes over South Africa at the expense of destroying the economic viability of South Africa will be a revolutionary government ousted by counter-revolution. We dare not propel South Africa in a direction in which we will face an endless cycle of revolution and counter-revolution.

I turn my back on all ideological thinking when I say that we cannot afford even to dabble with Marxist-type solutions for South Africa. No ideology can produce the kind of South Africa the people would be happy to live in if that ideology was not a workhorse for economic development. The sterile ideological conflicts of the past – from many sides – should now be abandoned. A Southern African perspective of today must be formulated from within today's circumstances.

We must get on with the tried and tested and we must do so as human beings living on the face of the earth who are created subject to the nature of man and the nature of society. We have a vast human history to look at beyond the history of Africa.

All human experience has led, I believe, to the values of democracy being underlined as the only sane and just values which can keep a country intact and functioning.

Politics of vision tailored for South African needs are imperative. This will require discipline in which rigorous thought, analysis and bold thinking is employed. This must be done now. We do not have the luxury of time in which we can indulge in a vast over-kill of apartheid, which is dying anyway, without planning what happens after apartheid.

We need to be looking specifically at economic questions relating to South Africa in conjunction with the broader context of Southern African imperatives. We must look at the salvation of South Africa in the context of Southern Africa.

There is an ongoing political and economic process happening daily in this country and black bargaining power has grown because of structural factors in politics and in society. You cannot have an expanding industrial economy in which the minority force are white and the majority are black. Economic expansion alone ensured that blacks escaped the fate of being drawers of water and hewers of wood.

Black South Africans have seen the extent to which economic imperatives have begun to accumulate to condemn apartheid from within. It was economic imperatives which resulted in the South African Government's reform programme; which motivated former State President P. W. Botha to do more to bring about change than any of his predecessors. Economic imperatives made black and white dependent on each other and this is precisely what apartheid was designed to avoid.

The growth of black bargaining power has passed the threshold beyond which it can any longer be countered by whites. There is a total white dependence on blacks. No city can be run without blacks. The country's entire productive process rests on blacks. It is not only black labour that is now needed. There are not enough white supervisors; there are not enough white technicians, there are not enough white experts in any field to ensure that the productive capacity of South Africa can be optimised.

Most significantly, perhaps, it is not only a question of relying on blacks to fill future jobs if the economy were to be optimised. Right now whites are dependent on blacks for the maintenance of their standards of living.

Black bargaining power has the leverage of this white dependence on blacks. It is a leverage which is particularly important because there is a counter-balancing black dependence on whites in the economy. Both black and white need each other. This means we have to learn to live with each other and I say we can.

It is important to note that not a factory in South Africa is closed now because black politics is intent on destroying the whole South African way of life, insofar as a future multi-party democracy in a free-enterprise system is concerned. Black politics does not want to do this. Black politics wants to enter the status quo and to transform it positively.

We need to do more than learn to live together in the sense of learning to tolerate each other. We have to strike up a partnership in which living together is a joint effort to conquer poverty, ignorance and disease.

We have to learn to live with each other in the pursuit of all those things that need to be done to ensure that there is finally total equality before the law and total equality of opportunity. The latter equality depends entirely on the first.

So I once again return to the reality that black and white in South Africa will really have to make what amounts to a national effort to succeed because a failure to conquer poverty, ignorance and disease will threaten us with a very bleak future.

There is so much in South Africa that needs to be handed with firmness and many stances that are uncompromising on vital issues will have to be struck. There are life-and-death issues at stake.

The time is ripe for innovative economic thinking and political action within South Africa and abroad. We need to start planning and we must be practical in our planning. The era of ideology is ending; it is time now for pragmatists to roll up their sleeves and start getting the job done.

The days are gone when white businessmen in South Africa did what the Government told them to do. In the country's organised mining, commerce, industry and banking, the interests of Afrikaans-speaking and English-speaking South Africans are becoming identical. Captains of industry now speak with one voice demanding a new South Africa.

They know now that by helping to perpetuate apartheid by adherence to racist labour practices and legislation, they were threatening the continuation of the free-enterprise system.

To a very real extent big business has said 'so far and no further.' The whole of mining, banking, commerce and industry is now gearing up to a post-apartheid South Africa in which there will be no racial exclusivity for whites. They are moving to a market dominated by black interests.

Commerce and industry no longer talks about whether there should be reform. There is a total readiness for reform. It is this readiness which makes it so tragic that we are not further along the road to drafting a new constitution and actually creating a new and positive future.

The 'quiet revolution' of Black South Africa

4

One of the greatest delusions in the world is the hope that the evils of this world can be cured by legislation
Speaker Thomas B. Reed, 1839–1902

In continuing my thoughts on the economy and black attitudes now and in a post-apartheid South Africa, I readily acknowledge why many of our trade union leaders and others espouse socialism of one kind or another.

Leaders of big business know only too well that this is because of the perceived and very real past relationship between capitalism and apartheid.

Dr Zach de Beer, a former director of the Anglo American Corporation, who has since returned to opposition politics, says he believes that big business has yet to demonstrate to workers that they have much to gain from free enterprise and that this can only be achieved through black advancement in commerce and industry, a fair wage policy and the provision of decent conditions for workers both in the workplace and outside.

I do not find it surprising at all when I see my own Anglican Archbishop, Desmond Tutu, quoted as saying that he hates capitalism. In an interview during a visit to Shanghai (*Business Day*, August 11, 1986) Archibishop Tutu told reporters: 'I abhor capitalism. The way the West has operated by and large in this matter of apartheid gives me no reason to want to change my views about capitalism. My own preference would be for some form of socialism.'

Mr Cyril Ramaphosa, Secretary-General of the National Union of Mineworkers, put it more bluntly in an interview with Michel

Albeldas and Alan Fischer (*A Question of Survival*, Jonathan Ball Publishers) when he was asked: 'Is there any trust between unions and big business?'

Mr Ramaphosa replied: 'Trust? Personally I do not trust any capitalist, because we operate on different wavelengths . . . I cannot trust a man who regards every person in the street as a labourer, who looks at every situation as one where he can make a profit . . . I feel that most of the union leaders do not trust the capitalists.'

In an interview for the same book, Mr Phiroshaw Camay, Secretary-General of the Council of Unions of South Africa, was asked: 'Do you think today that most blacks in South Africa prefer a socialist economic and political system to a capitalist one?'

Mr Camay replied: 'Well, I think that what is happening right now is that people are saying that apartheid is synonymous with capitalism. And so, because apartheid is a bad system, capitalism is also bad. People are mouthing slogans about socialism while not really understanding what they mean by socialism or a one-party state system.'

When the authors of this book asked me the same question, I answered: 'I know that there are organisations that are talking about a socialist future. But in fact, it is the theoreticians in these organisations that are selling this idea. On the whole, black people in their hundreds of thousands are working in the free-enterprise system. I don't think that one can say at the moment that black people don't want a free-enterprise system. I believe it is really premature to perceive that perhaps we want a socialist system. I believe that blacks in this country, even those like myself who admired socialism at some time in their lives, would find that the realities of the situation tell us that we do not know of any other system which is as potent a force for development as the free-enterprise capitalist system.'

I added my feelings, as they still stand today, that I was extremely anxious that not enough blacks were entering the free-enterprise system and that they *must* be given points of entry. If black people don't feel a part of the free-enterprise system, they will reject it. It is as simple as that.

Big business, by and large, has accepted the need for rapid black advancement. The Anglo American Corporation say they are working towards the goal of equal opportunity as well as adapting to the needs and aspirations of a new South African society. What business *per se* is doing, across the board, is another matter entirely and there is no doubt that whatever programmes exist must be accelerated. Even what they say they are trying to do is not enough.

Mr Gavin Relly, the chairman of Anglo American, believes that South Africa, with all its controls, is not a good example of a free-enterprise economy and much more must be done in 'selling' it to South Africans. 'A free-enterprise economic system is a goal for which we are currently striving and it carries with it the vital complementary concept of free choice,' he says.

Reforms, he adds, should not be confined to the political field but should be extended to the business sector. Businessmen should advance non-racial interaction for the purpose of facilitating economic growth and for the interests of society as a whole.

Meanwhile, what are ordinary blacks doing now in South Africa's economy and in our cities, towns and villages? Shouldn't their current efforts be a pointer towards our future?

Believing, as I have said, that politics and economics are inextricably interwoven, it is already acknowledged that not politicians, not trade union leaders, not churchmen but ordinary black men and women have, in an almost silent revolution, changed the political and economic face of South Africa.

In defiance of the Group Areas Act, millions of blacks have packed up and moved from where apartheid had herded them for so many generations. So-called 'white' cities have become black almost overnight with huge black settlements on or immediately around their borders. Others have set up residence in former 'whites only' apartment buildings and in city suburbs.

Nothing short of a massive assault of sheer naked power from the forces of racism may dislodge blacks temporarily from these and other areas. I doubt if this kind of brutality would ever succeed because it would be a human outrage and simply impossible. Some say that the government has to all intents and purposes abandoned efforts to remove them. I hope so.

These black men and women, together with their children, have changed the face of apartheid in South Africa for good. They have won with stealth, determination and courage.

The next step is, of course, that they will demand – as they should – that they contribute to the running of these areas and it is only a matter of time before they will. Here one will see how social change will spill over into the political field.

It is estimated that at the moment blacks account for only half the country's urban population but by the end of the century they will outnumber whites three to one.

The Executive Director of the South African Institute of Race Relations (SAIRR), Mr John Kane-Berman, in a speech in Amsterdam (*The Natal Mercury*, June 20, 1989), aptly described local government as the 'soft underbelly' of political apartheid.

Mr Kane-Berman described how more than half the residents of Johannesburg's supposedly white central business district are black people living there illegally, while R7 out of every R10 spent in downtown Johannesburg comes out of black pockets.

'It is fanciful to think that this city, which is becoming blacker by the day, can continue to be run indefinitely by a lily-white city council,' Mr Kane-Berman said. 'Local authorities are likely to learn a lesson learned long ago by employers in their factories: you cannot run a city properly if you hold yourself accountable only to white residents, who constitute an ever-diminishing proportion of the people under your jurisdiction, any more than you can run a factory properly if you talk only to white trade unions and ignore black unions.'

Black workers began, more than two decades ago, asserting their rights in their places of employment. Through strikes and the mobilisation of trade unions, employers learnt the hard way that to survive, across-the-board dialogue was a crucial necessity. If whites wanted their factories to operate, they had to negotiate with blacks.

Step by step, black South Africans have infiltrated white political, social and economic domains.

Again Mr Kane-Berman summed it up when he told his audience in Amsterdam: 'Post-apartheid South Africa is not something that will be legislated into existence by some future government: It is already being created on the ground, to a large extent by the actions of ordinary people who have made apartheid laws unworkable.'

When drafting this book, my vision of the future of South Africa, I obviously looked to what others were also saying. Too often in this country it is only those with political agendas that are heard and I wanted, here, to express what ordinary black men and women are doing. Their efforts have been, in fact, extraordinary and South Africa's future is being shaped by them in what has been described as a silent revolution.

This revolution is taking place today in cities and towns, factories, shops, schools, universities, in public transport, on beaches and in cinemas. Everything that is taking place is propelling this country towards a multi-racial future in which blacks have already shown, to a very large degree, that given the opportunity they are willing participants in the free-enterprise system.

The SAIRR has isolated a number of extremely important components in this so-called silent revolution which to me aptly reveal how ordinary blacks are, as I have emphasised so often, themselves dismantling apartheid peacefully and constructively infiltrating previously white-dominated social and economic domains. They are freely and actively involving themselves in free enterprise whenever they can. This augurs well for the future and should be a source of inspiration to those who seek a secure and prosperous future for this country.

It should also be a clear message to revolutionaries. In all that they have been doing, black South Africans did not need guns, orchestrated upheavals and rigid ideological instuctions from political activists; all they needed was a determination to annihilate apartheid in their own way, which they have in abundance.

In a document prepared by Mr Kane-Berman he outlined the 'profound process' of this silent revolution. I have extracted the following points which clearly show that the actions of ordinary men and women have been accompanied by the steady erosion of apartheid:

The Group Areas Act:
Various estimates put the number of black people unlawfully resident in white areas at between 100,000 and 250,000. Another example of how change in South Africa is being brought about by the man in the street rather than the political leadership . . . People are just moving into Hillbrow in Johannesburg, Woodstock in Cape Town and white suburbs elsewhere in the country despite what the law says.

The Pass Laws:
Yet another instance of the erosion of apartheid is the fate of the Pass Laws which were repealed in 1986, not because the government wanted to, but because they were unworkable. Black South Africans simply refused to remain where they were told and despite the risk of arrest and prosecution repeatedly returned to

settle and work in so-called 'white' areas. Crossroads, a huge squatter settlement in Cape Town, is a classic example. Year in and year out the authorities tried to remove the people and send them back to the Ciskei and the Transkei. They simply got off the buses or the trains and went straight back to Cape Town so that eventually the authorities threw in the towel and allowed Crossroads to remain. These blacks simply, and powerfully, voted with their feet.

Urbanisation:

South Africa is getting to the stage where the urban population is overtaking the rural population in size for the first time. Durban, for example, is one of the fastest growing cities in the world, with an increase every year in the region of 8 per cent. On that growth trend, Durban in the year 2000 is going to have as many people as Greater London has today. One of the implications of large-scale urbanisation is concentrated markets for consumer goods. At the moment urban blacks and whites are roughly balanced in numbers but by the year 2000 black people will outnumber whites in the cities by 3 to 1.

Education:

Between 1955 and the year 2000 the increase in the number of Africans taking matriculation examinations will have been on present trends no less than 40,000 per cent. At the moment about half of all people taking matriculation in this country are black. In the year 2000 seven out of every ten matriculants are going to be black. One can already see how this is changing the racial composition of higher education. In 1966, 11 per cent of university students in South Africa were black; in 1986 the figure was 40 per cent. This is already having important consequences for the profile of the country's middle-level manpower. In 1965 it was 20 per cent black, in 1985 it was 40 per cent black. The changing composition of the country's intellectual capital is an extremely important component of the silent revolution. Universities are now free to decide their own admission policy and private schools are effectively desegregated. More recently technikons have been free from racial restrictions laid down by the government on who may attend them. It is probably a reasonable prediction that within the next few years white teacher training colleges, at the moment rigidly segregated, are going to be given some leeway in admitting people of other races.

56

Consumer spending:
One example is liquor. Eighty per cent of all liquor consumed in South Africa is consumed by black people. Africans in the Pretoria/Witwatersrand/Vereeniging area alone consume more liquor every day than whites in the whole country. *Castle* is one of the top-selling of beers in the world, due almost entirely to the fact that it is the beer that black people in South Africa prefer. The Avis car hire company has opened its first depot in a black area, Soweto. Black families are now hiring cars on weekend specials – a completely new phenomenon for the car hire business here. Another interesting statistic is that between 85 and 95 per cent of weekend spending in Johannesburg's up-market Carlton Centre shops comes out of black pockets.

Income distribution:
In 1960 whites accounted for 63 per cent of all disposable income in South Africa but by the year 2000 the white share will be down to 43 per cent.

Housing:
In 1982, 13 per cent of the building plans passed by local authorities were for black housing but in 1988 the figure was 57 per cent. One building society reported that a quarter of all the home lending was now being accounted for by black people. The small black building entrepreneur is going to be a major success story in the black business community.

Black taxis:
According to some analysts the investment in this industry is equivalent to that of two major gold mines and the employment generated by black taxis is as much as is provided by ten gold mines. It is also said that the consumption every day of petrol by the black taxi industry is second only to consumption by the government itself. The black taxi industry has started to elbow aside established sections of the transport business. The Southern Africa Black Taxi Association (SABTA) has recently tendered to provide a taxi service for whites in the exclusive white suburb of Sandton, near Johannesburg. It is now thinking of going multi-national and offering to provide a taxi service in Maputo, Mozambique. Taxis are beginning to play an influential role in determining transport to shopping centres in Soweto and elsewhere. In Pietersburg in the northern Transvaal, the town council

recently refused to establish a black taxi rank in the town but the three major supermarkets there are now competing with one another to provide taxi ranks next to their stores because they want the business that the taxis will bring to them from the black neighbouring townships. The supermarkets know something that the town council does not know: that their future depends on attracting black custom.

Trade Unions:
Only a few years ago 250,000 workers in South Africa were members of multiracial trade unions. The figure is now 1.5 million. In the 1970s black unions were not illegal but the government did not like them and they had no statutory protection or official status. Starting in the Durban/Pinetown area at the end of 1972/73 and then spreading to the rest of the country, black workers in their tens of thousands joined the unions anyway. They did so despite victimisation by employers and harassment by the security police. Eventually the government recognised that black unions were a phenomenon that had come to stay and granted them the statutory status they had been seeking.

Mr Kane-Berman makes the point that this silent revolution was not something brought about by political élites but by the ordinary man, woman and sometimes the child in the street.

Ordinary black South Africans are not following but leading the Government and political activists and in so doing are transforming the country socially and economically. All that the Government can do now is to try to contain this onward march, but they won't succeed. The changes are irreversible, as the people of Boksburg are now finding out the hard way, when their white Conservative Party council tried to turn the clock back to apartheid's rigidly segregated days.

What black people in this area did was to boycott white shops and send many concerns bankrupt.

Most of the changes in South Africa have occurred on the ground first, and only thereafter has parliament legislated to cater for the new reality. At the moment, for instance, parliament is considering legislation that will legalise the position of black people in certain *de facto* mixed areas in the country. The amendments to liberalise the Group Areas Act are coming about only because in many areas it has ceased to operate.

Again Mr Kane-Berman notes: 'The strategic implication for

Mangosuthu G. Buthelezi.

Meeting with Prime Minister Margaret Thatcher and the South African author Sir Lawrence van der Post (top).

In conversation with the industrialist Harry F. Oppenheimer (above).

Meeting with West German colleagues: Chancellor Helmut Kohl (above) and the Minister for Overseas Development, Warncke (below).

A warm handshake for Ex-President Ronald Reagan.

*n exchange of opinions with the President of the United States, George Bush (above), and with
e Mayor of Los Angeles, Tom Bradley (below).*

Lively conversations with South Africa's renowned author Alan Paton (above), and with the Black American Presidential candidate Jesse Jackson (below).

OPPOSITE
Meeting with the German Foreign Minister, Hans-Dietrich Genscher (above), and his former office colleague Shimon Perez (below).

On good terms with the Archbishop of Canterbury, Dr Robert Runcie.

people who want to work for change in this country is not to go around begging the government to do certain things, but just to do it yourself as people did with the Group Areas Act, with unions, with Pass Laws and so on. You can be fairly confident that if you create a new situation on the ground the government will soon change the legislation to cater for the new reality which you have brought into being.'

Quite obviously this process of socio-economic change is going to advance into the political field and is already doing so. The Government has had to retreat from official apartheid policy time and again and will have to continue to do so.

In a newspaper article the Minister of Law and Order, Mr Adriaan Vlok, was quoted at a public meeting in Standerton as saying that 'fighting for apartheid was a lost cause.' Mr Vlok added: 'This is the viewpoint of the National Party and I believe in it too. Apartheid is no longer the policy of the National Party.' The National Party would 'go for the moderates' in trying to reach a political solution that was acceptable to the majority of reasonable people. The National Party needed a mandate from the electorate to work out a new constitutional dispensation with moderate and reasonable people. This would not be easy because the government would have to negotiate with people who 'feel wronged by events of the past . . .' (*The Citizen*, August 1, 1989).

Even three years ago, statements such as this from a Government minister would have been unthinkable.

The Government is admitting that it does not have the power to maintain apartheid and crush black resistance – even with continuing states of emergency. Apartheid is being stripped away from the body politic of South Africa layer by layer. Old apartheid ideologies of blacks being temporary sojourners in so-called white areas, with the economy being built on black migrant labour, have become an outdated farce.

One frequently hears statements about how complex the South African situation is, because the situation is indeed complex. Complexity, however, does not defy analysis. Right courses of action in simple issues are either/or courses of action. In complex situations the right thing itself is often not so simple. We have to be conscious of the need to think our way through complexity and that often takes time. Having come to grips with a complex situation, one is then more often than not in an advantageous position of having a multiple choice to make between many things, all of which are good and constructive.

It is the complexity of the South African situation which provides that a diversity of inputs can be made to assist in bringing about change. The actions of ordinary men and women, as described, illustrate this.

As a black leader, I therefore see the complexity of the South African situation as a challenge that can be met. We must, however, get a number of things straight before we do so.

The first thing I think we should do when we consider South Africa at large, and in a post-apartheid era, is to focus on the time element. The need to do so is very apparent when one realises the extent to which black South Africans in their masses are totally convinced that apartheid is doomed and that we will have a new society with political rights for all. For us apartheid is not invincible and I have tried to show this in describing some of the actions, to date, of ordinary black men and women.

We have both chipped away and smashed away at the granite facade of apartheid as it was in its earlier decades of existence.

Afrikanerdom is no longer monolithic. The National Party is not only irreconcilably opposed to the right-wing Conservative Party, and vice versa but inside the National Party *verligt* (enlightened) and the *verkrampt* (closed) factions vie with each other to direct the policy of the State from within the National Party caucus.

As blacks we know that it is just a pure pipedream for whites to believe that there will be any unscrambling of the total inter-dependence between black and white in the economic field. We know this gives us negotiating power which can only increase as white dependence on blacks – which is already there – becomes an overwhelming political factor. Economic interdependence must lead to political interdependence. We know that.

When I talk about the need to focus on time, I point to these realities and say that there is a time lag between realities on the ground in South Africa and perceptions of them. I would put the media, in general, something like two years behind the movement of real politics in this country. They can capture what a politician does today. The media have proved hopeless in predicting what is going to happen in politics tomorrow.

The battle for trade union rights for blacks was not won on the day that legislation was amended to make trade unions for blacks effectively operative. The battle was not won on the day on which a commission was appointed by the Government to go into the whole question of black trade unionism. The battle for black trade union rights was won before that; these things were all the consequences of victory – the consummation of battles won.

If you read press reports of black trade unionism prior to the appointment of the Wiehan Commission you will find that the press was unaware of the extent to which there would be capitulation on the part of the Government.

If you look at the 1975/77 period you will find that the press in South Africa, and the foreign press for that matter, in the first place did not predict the upheavals of 1976 and 1977, and once these upheavals had erupted to astound them they presented a South Africa in which the Government was on the run from unstoppable unrest and violence. In 1977 the press did not predict the commanding position the Government would hold in 1979.

There is an absolute dearth of analytical journalism in South Africa. The media lives on a day-to-day diet and there is an ever-present tendency to report the dramatic. The dramatic is what is saleable and it is saleable whether it proves previous dramatic stories were far-fetched or not.

We again had this phenomena emerging in the 1983/84 period when many people in Western Europe, North America and elsewhere perceived South Africa going up in flames, with the violent Left marching unstoppably forward. It is these perceptions which live on even when events quieten down. And when people forget the detail of the drama reported, they are left with background impressions which continue to work away regardless of what is actually happening in South Africa.

The whole disinvestment scene is one in which this kind of thing is happening. It was the drama of 1983–5 leading to the sensational reporting – and President Kenneth Kaunda's warning of holocausts and blood-baths – that fired the decisions made in board rooms to disinvest. It was the drama which politicians picked up in Africa and elsewhere in the Third World as sticks with which to beat the West which further internationalised the whole question of whether to disinvest or not.

The fact that apartheid has run out of steam and the fact that the Government can go nowhere without black cooperation are irrelevant to some. It's as if some are blind, unable to see that sooner rather than later apartheid is finally going to crumble.

I don't know exactly when apartheid is finally going to be

declared dead and buried; nobody does. I don't know exactly when the day of our total freedom will come. I do know that it will come in the not-too-distant future. I see our liberation as a process which will culminate in meaningful negotiations.

My prayers and thoughts long into most nights are that we are left alone long enough to peacefully achieve this.

Now is the time for black and white South Africans to be given the chance to develop tactics and strategies in planning a post-apartheid future acceptable to all. We don't need external threats, we don't need crippling sanctions and disinvestment which will only set back our post-apartheid recovery efforts.

The glib media treatment of the drama in today's news does not unearth the basic ongoing political process in the country, so ably described by the S.A. Institute of Race Relations and others.

In that process black bargaining power has grown because of structural factors in politics and in society. The normal distribution of skills and aptitudes are there in black society as well as white society and when efficiency demanded merit, blacks with the right skills had to be brought in and had to be trained.

The Apprenticeship Act had to be scrapped and the regimentation of migrant labour had to be abandoned in favour of scrapping Pass Laws and Influx Control regulations. Black mobility came with black skills and the *de facto* black presence in so-called white cities made nonsense of apartheid's dreams.

All sorts of factors began evolving outside the view of the drama-hungry media. Black society began changing and there was an outreach by black to black across all the barriers apartheid has attempted to establish not only between black and white but between black and black as well. Everywhere, nuclei around which black bargaining power would begin to evolve came into existence. I now actually laugh to myself when the Government is sometimes so earnest in presenting plans for what I know to be impossible.

The Tricameral parliamentary system cannot work now and it had no chance of working right from the beginning. It has radicalised black politics. It has deepened black anger and it has brought no political gains for whites. I now know beyond all shadow of doubt that the present constitution will be scrapped. I know that the ruling National Party already knows this but the national and international media continue reporting as though this is a battle still to be won. It is already won in the sense that we now know that the scrapping of the constitution is inevitable. It was won because blacks opposed it and now the Government is talking about a new constitution.

All that sanctions and other measures inhibiting black advancement can now do, is to curb the underlying political process in which black bargaining power has been growing and apartheid has been rolled into a precarious political existence. I am not saying that the struggle for liberation has been won and I repeat this over and over again. There are tough times ahead. All I am saying is that we are ready for that toughness and we know that it will be the toughness of the final push to victory.

This is not idealism or wishful thinking. It is political realism. I know that the politics of negotiation is going to succeed because when I look around me I see the armed struggle having failed and continuing to fail as far as we can see ahead. Already the Soviet Union, the United States, Cuba and Angola have accepted that Southern African issues cannot be settled through violence.

Equally crucial is also the acceptance now elsewhere in Southern Africa of the need for free enterprise in attempts to restore economies ravaged by war and socialist planning gone wrong.

When I write that South Africa – and indeed Southern Africa – is complex, I ask you to take what I say about time seriously and to look, as I do, at structural realities in politics and in society at large rather than be guided by the short-term view of the media.

The vast majority of black South Africans are intent, as I have attempted to show, in gaining entry into all those areas whites want to keep sacrosanct unto themselves and, once involved, to build and not to destroy. They want to do so peacefully and are showing this by their actions.

The clear message from black South Africa is that people want more jobs, more investment and more participation in wealth creation and the profits thereof. This means involving themselves in a free-enterprise system and not with what socialism may or may not have in store for them.

Inkatha, with its vast numbers of black members and supporters drawn from all walks of black society, passed a resolution at one of its recent conferences which illustrates this:

'We believe that the resources of the country and the wealth which has already been created which is controlled by the State, belongs to all the people of South Africa, and we believe that the resources and the wealth of the country should be utilised for the greater good of the greater number . . .'

A Statement of Belief endorsed by the movement added: 'We believe that we are facing a grave crisis in which the poor are threatened with greater poverty and we believe it is essential that all men join hands and enter into a partnership with the State to effect the greatest possible redistribution of wealth commensurate with maximising the productivity of commerce, trade and industry whether State-controlled or privately owned.'

Inkatha believes that a redistribution of the total wealth of South Africa can only be achieved by the redistribution of the opportunity to create wealth and the redistribution of opportunity to benefit from wealth.

For Inkatha the problem is no longer whether a future South Africa will embrace the free-enterprise system or socialism. The question is what needs to be done to make the free-enterprise system acceptable to the greatest number of South Africans – black and white – now.

Research and reality has shown that capitalism in developed countries is much more than simply an economic system through a certain mode of production. The capitalist free-enterprise democracy is a social system that meets certain conditions and for the benefit of my brothers and sisters in South and Southern Africa who may be unfamiliar with them, I would like to list them:

> Free elections
> Freedom of political association
> Freedom of religion, thought and speech
> Equality before the law
> The right to oppose the government
> The right to choose one's job
> The right to form trade unions
> The right to move freely
> Firms or countries have the freedom to produce, sell and distribute their goods and services.

The basic characteristics of a capitalist free-enterprise democracy therefore emphasise the rights of the individual and these liberal democratic principles are related to liberty and the pursuit of happiness.

Socialism has been defined many ways; J. A. Schumpeter (*Capitalism, Socialism and Democracy* – London, Unwin Hyman Ltd., 1987) wrote: 'By socialist society we shall designate an institutional pattern in which the control over the means of production itself is vested with a central authority or, as we may say, in which, as a matter of principle, the economic affairs of society belong to the public and not to the private sector.'

The long list of the failures of socialism to deliver the goods to the masses in Africa and elsewhere and to bring about stable, democratic countries must be acknowledged and is in the process of, finally, being openly and honestly admitted by some.

By espousing a capitalist free-enterprise democracy, Inkatha strongly believes in the notion that all people are equal before God and therefore this equality must be rooted in the liberal democratic free-enterprise tradition itself.

We all know, as I started off by saying, that some blacks believe that a capitalist democracy has no future in a post-apartheid South Africa because they see apartheid and capitalism as synonymous.

Apartheid laws have done away with the equality and freedom necessary for a capitalist free-enterprise democracy.

Therefore I say that a capitalist free-enterprise system for South Africa needs to be re-worked, re-elaborated and put into practice. Capitalism in South Africa must be seen in its true form, as synonymous with a truly democratic and non-racial society. We must not allow apartheid as practised in present-day South Africa to force us to throw away the free-enterprise baby with the bath water.

Black disunity

5

Behold how good and joyful
   a thing it is, brethren,
to dwell together in unity.
      Book of Common Prayer

*I*t is a central argument in my whole political position now that forces working for change in South Africa are being detrimentally affected by black disunity. Part of the hideousness of apartheid is that it has precipitated internecine black conflict. Democratic politics requires democratic institutions in which values and norms are upheld and in which decent behaviour prevails. Right now in South Africa, in black politics particularly, it is as if we are in the midst of an acrimonious taproom free-for-all. Delays in black unity are simply heaping up the cost of the final victory which is inevitably going to be ours.

Black South Africa has been denied the right to evolve its own democratic machinery and forces. As a result, racists in South Africa and elsewhere laugh openly because we black people are attacking each other daily. This is something which distresses me greatly, and I weep not only for the men, women and children in Inkatha's ranks whom we have buried over the years.

Black disunity upsets me more than anything else because it shows weakness and it shames us. It makes a mockery of our combined cultural and spiritual forces, at the core of which is African humanism and respect for one another.

The loss of thousands of lives over the years of supporters of various political organisations, or their affiliates, and many innocents caught up in the whirlwinds that have been sown, is a human tragedy with far-reaching implications.

Apart from the senseless killing, we are snarling at each other from public platforms and a ghastly atmosphere of intolerance has proliferated among some who seem to apply the dictum: 'If you are not with us, you are against us.' Groups and individuals abroad have joined in and taken sides, further exacerbating this unhealthy situation.

While we must accept that there is conflict – mainly over anti-apartheid tactics and strategies and post-apartheid constitutional and socio-economic positions – we all have a responsibility to defuse what is happening. We must all meet and talk about our differences.

The thing most dominant about South Africa today from a political point of view is the rise of forces which are no longer seeking a democratic solution to this country's problems. Even though the vast majority seek peaceful democratic change, black South Africans are, nevertheless, being encouraged by some to kill and destroy for political purposes.

The politics of intimidation has been on the ascendancy for some time now and everywhere in the country democratic forces working through non-violent tactics and strategies to bring about change through negotiation are under siege.

Divisiveness on the black political front is crippling us. While black politics remain shackled by a lack of basic political freedoms, consensus politics will not evolve. We blacks can only evolve consensus opinions if we have the democratic machinery to produce them. South African laws and administrative action, together with white political drives, have always acted to fragment black democracy.

This being the case, I have always argued for a multi-strategy approach in which each organisation can do what it best can do in its own circumstances – and a correct division of responsibility between civil, cultural, political, labour and religious movements. Our common enemy is, after all, apartheid and it has now become imperative that black South Africans come together, bury past differences as intelligently as they can, and utilise various democratic tactics and strategies for the common good.

A multi-strategy approach is an open-ended approach. It does not forward any political party as being pre-eminent and it does not insist on political regimentation, conformity or any particular discipline of thought. The emphasis is on tolerance and a means by which all, in their own way, can collectively work for what they believe is best for the country and for themselves.

Divide and rule policies of successive National Party Governments have always attempted to smash any black democratic forces of consequence and the Government is now facing the fact that there is nobody who will negotiate with it in the present circumstances.

The black democratic body politic in South Africa must emerge as healthy and intact for the negotiations that will come. We must restore black solidarity and we must start doing it now.

Decade after decade of black opposition to apartheid has clearly shown that there is no single black political organisation capable of winning the black struggle for liberation.

Individuals and organisations within South Africa and abroad must now see the need for compromise and to accept that a multi-strategy approach does, in fact, go hand in hand with democratic options.

In Inkatha and KwaZulu, for instance, we have never claimed to be the sole and authentic voice of black South Africa. We welcome divergent views and respect the right of all South Africans to present their views to the masses.

If we are to achieve an interim position from which we can launch the final shaping of South Africa, black South Africans *must* consider alternative compromise formulae which are not based solely on the winner-takes-all demand. Black democratic consensus cannot evolve in isolation. Whites have failed to solve the country's problems unilaterally and blacks too will fail if they attempt to do so unilaterally.

South Africa has a multi-racial future and we should be committed to the development of black democracy as part of a wider multi-racial democracy. History has intertwined black and white destinies in this country. We have a shared destiny which demands a shared responsibility between black and white.

Black people will compromise if black compromises are met with white compromises. At the same time, blacks must compromise with each other. No one black political organisation will ever win the fight to rid this country of racism and build a new and united future. The only victory that there will ever be is a people's victory.

People support organisations of a wide variety. They support each organisation for what that organisation can best do in its own circumstances. That is why I am convinced that there must be a division of labour in the struggle for liberation and support a multi-strategy approach. It is the only approach which the people themselves have got. They employ that approach every day of their lives which I have attempted to portray in previous chapters. That approach is the only approach that will give us black unity.

Power is the people's power and the people must decide who should lead them and in what direction they wish to be led. We all have one destiny and that is why it is so vitally important for us to develop consensus and unity. We must stop allowing problems over tactics and strategies to divide us so tragically.

Black political strength and black revulsion of apartheid in South Africa is, to a large degree, being squandered and in the process of articulating black anger, uncoordinated groups have found themselves crushed time after time by the State. Because victory is inevitable, I call for all blacks to unite for that final push to democratic victory. Beyond that victory lies the need for massive national South African unity if the country is ever going to make the successful outcome of the struggle meaningful to the masses.

Internecine black strife threatens black democracy. The politics of violence and intimidation threaten black democracy. Mass poverty, ignorance and disease threaten democracy.

There is right now a raging battle for minds taking place in South Africa. This has been the theme of many of my addresses for quite some time and it also flows through this book. The free-enterprise system is at stake; multi-party democracy as it is known in the Western world is at stake.

Conflicting forces are seeking alternative ends in authoring the future of South Africa and this intense awareness that what we do and how we do it will bring about radical change makes for very turbulent politics.

How we remove apartheid, what tactics and strategies we employ, who we ally ourselves with as we do, is going to determine the kind of society we will have after apartheid. Life and death issues are involved.

On one side of a deepening polarisation in black South Africa are those who want to establish a socialist one-party State. On the other side are those who want to establish a multi-party free-enterprise democracy. In the former, tactics and strategies designed to bring about the eradication of apartheid are also designed to produce the conformity of thought which disciplined revolutionaries believe they have the right to impose on people. Those who seek multi-party democracy seek the destruction of apartheid in tactics and strategies which are designed to set the people free to do their own choosing and to author their own destiny.

I have never said that those who have chosen to adopt the tactics and strategies of the armed struggle did not have a right to make that decision, however much I abhor violence. I accept that apartheid has pushed many people beyond human endurance. In the same way I believe I have the right to insist that others should respect my decision and those of my supporters and millions of others, to seek liberation through a process of meaningful change, negotiation and non-violence.

Now is the time for courage and we must not lose it. We must not now, at this point in time, throw up our hands in despair, get angry, and just smash anything and everything to get rid of apartheid. That for me would be the final victory of apartheid – the destruction of the foundations of the future.

There is no magic in politics. The future will not be secured if we simply destroy apartheid. I can think of a great many countries where there is no apartheid in which I could not even think of living. There have been many political victories against colonialism and against racism which have left the people in a parlous state of suffering. We must therefore act against apartheid while acting for democracy. Acting against apartheid is not automatically acting for democracy and unfortunately a great many people have been caught up in the latter action.

It is now totally irrelevant that some revolutionaries continue to call for the intensification of the armed struggle against South Africa. What is relevant to me is not what people talk about but what is actually happening. There is a move towards peace in South and Southern Africa and it is peace that we must seek because it is peace that will bring us nationhood.

There is a feeling in the world at large that mankind must now move to eliminate conflict areas and to establish the supremacy of diplomacy based on negotiation. This feeling has been emerging for some time now but it is beginning to crystallise and take on new shapes and forms. It is reaching out into Africa and the spirit of negotiation is now in the African air and is penetrating South African politics.

At a meeting of the Organisation of African Unity in 1989 the current chairman, Egyptian President Mr Hosni Mubarak, stated that African states must remain 'open-minded to every serious call for peace' and should not work in isolation but should be responsive to the international trend towards dialogue instead of confrontation.

He called on African states to approve a common step-by-step approach to resolving the South African issue, and for opposing black political groups to reconcile their differences. (*The Star*, August 21, 1989).

For some, however, it must be borne in mind that political reform – even reform judged to be meaningful by Western governments – threatens their interests. Some do not want the process of peaceful change resulting in negotiation to work. They talk in terms of power being handed over to the people or they attempt to dictate who may ultimately be involved in negotiations and who should be excluded – obviously to their own advantage. They use smear tactics to vilify all those whom they perceive to be their opponents. In the process they divide black from black and black from white.

It makes no sense but it is happening and it is ugly. I write from bitter and unhappy experience but it is no use my now going over propaganda which has been deeply wounding, wrong and destructive from whatever quarter. I cannot dwell on the past and fulminate over what was said yesterday and will no doubt be said again tomorrow.

I refuse to be a party to heightening tensions in a never-ending cycle of recriminations. I will defend myself and my supporters and put forward our aims and objectives as best and as forcefully as I can, as I have an obligation to do, but at the same time I want the hatred to cease and I want us to reach out to each other and to learn to live together with tolerance and with a united vision of hope for this country and a caring for one another.

Quite often when I meet various people internationally, from all walks of life, who have become involved in issues in South and Southern Africa, my heart warms to their open-mindedness and compassion. They steer clear of taking sides as far as anti-apartheid forces are concerned and they listen attentively and with wisdom. They may not agree with me on some or even many points, but they do not turn their backs either. They debate, each in their own way, with a mixture of awesome clarity, great scholarship and experience, humility, despair and humour. They care and they want to do what they can, whatever their expertise.

They too find apartheid revolting and the complexities of the situation taxing at the best of times. They offer hands of friendship and constructive dialogue. Quite often they go further and seek ways for us all to widen our horizons in areas in which we should.

None pretends to have all the answers. Equally encouraging is that they seek to extend humanitarian aid for my people that will transcend party political considerations and political advantages.

Whether we ultimately agree or disagree in our political discussions, I see them as powerful allies because we can work together, we can seek alternatives and we respect each other. We can build on what we have.

I also meet others who have hard eyes and closed, rigid minds. They refuse to listen to me or even accept that I have the right to my own point of view. They try to deny me platforms both within my own country and abroad. They sneer at what I attempt to project as worthless and they use the resources at their disposal to ruthlessly pillory me.

Sometimes they listen with half an ear, only waiting for the opportunity to attempt to smash me to the ground with damning and vile accusations; trying to goad me into never-ending bitter retorts resulting in counter-accusations. That's politics, we all know, but when you have been on the receiving end for as long as I have, and you have to live and work in the circumstances which apartheid has produced, it makes you tired to the bone.

I can take it, for the most part, and I respond when I feel I must, even though there are other things far more pressing to do. Those of us involved on the ground in the struggle owe it to history and to generations to come to try to set the record straight when we can. I write, I talk, I open my doors to all.

And they come. Into my office and even my home. They insult me, they distress my family. They arrive with fake smiles and leave with snarls and threats. They connive behind my back and plot my downfall. Even worse, they threaten the lives of those I dearly love. They treat the millions of people in KwaZulu as though they were lepers and they actively work to exclude them from the benefits of international funding for black empowerment. If only they would understand that I respect their right to differ with me.

A lifetime in politics does not make for perfection at all times. Great strides are made, mistakes are made. I have had to make the kind of gut-wrenching decisions that all who have been given authority must do when various situations arise. One makes friends and also enemies.

In South Africa today, and abroad, feelings run deep on a myriad of levels about our situation. Rational and informed debate on political issues is virtually non-existent and positions are so polarised that protagonists of various organisations rarely speak to each other, if ever. It is time for a change of heart all round. I am not calling for a capitulation of respective aims and objectives, I am calling over and over again for decency and democratic behaviour.

So, too, is our hero and martyr Dr Nelson Mandela. In a personal letter to me from his Victor Verster Prison quarters early in 1989, Dr Mandela said, in part: 'The most challenging task facing the leadership today is that of national unity. At no other time in our history has it become so crucial for our people to speak with one voice, and to pool their efforts. Any act or statement, from whatever source, which tends to create or worsen divisions is, in the existing political situation, a fatal error which ought to be avoided at all costs . . .

'In my entire political career few things have distressed me as to see our people killing one another as is now happening. As you know, the entire fabric of community life in some of the affected areas has been seriously disrupted, leaving behind a legacy of hatred and bitterness which may haunt us for years to come. It is a matter which requires the urgent attention of all people in this country. Nothing will please me more than to know that my concern and appeal have not fallen on deaf ears.'

He added that 'in due course' it was his fervent hope to see the 'restoration of the cordial relations which existed' between myself and the exiled President of the ANC, Mr Oliver Tambo, and between Inkatha and the ANC. He accepts the right of Inkatha to exist as much as the ANC to exist.

Dr Mandela wrote these words as a patriot and a true son of Africa. I can do no more than to attempt to spread his message both nationally and internationally.

For some people opposition to apartheid has been a chance for personal, political and other gain, both within South Africa and internationally. They have used the oppression of millions of blacks in this country to create specific platforms and advantages for themselves in their own countries and here I am thinking, in particular, of certain politicians and political ideologues, lobbyists and other so-called activists in the United States, Europe and elsewhere.

Black South Africa welcomes the genuine disgust of apartheid displayed by many well-meaning opponents of our situation abroad and all that they attempt to do to alleviate black suffering.

Having been in politics for so long in this country I cannot be naive about the selfish and somewhat cynical motivations of some who often do not give two hoots about the ordinary black man, woman and child in South Africa. They, too, have their own agendas.

I am reminded here, in part, of a commentary in the *Sunday Times* (August 6, 1989) in which the author noted: 'The truth is that the international anti-apartheid movement (AAM) has become a cottage industry whose continued existence depends on the continued existence of apartheid, just as the existence of the insurance industry depends on the continued occurrence of fires, accidents and the like.

'The AAM has a vested interest in denying that any change has taken place in South Africa. Indeed, it seems as if the AAM regards successful blows against apartheid not as victories but as threats to itself. The usefulness of international pressure is diminished, if not negated, if its response to concessions is not reward, but indiscriminate punishment that throws the baby out with the bath water.

'The AAM has long held the moral high ground. But refusal to recognise that South Africa is changing is eroding its position . . . The AAM's all-or-nothing approach seeks to deny the fact that peaceful change is not only possible but is actually happening in South Africa in fields far wider than sport. Worst of all, it spurns all the evidence that the victims of apartheid by their own actions are demonstrating their ability to change South Africa in a non-violent way . . .'

In quoting this I am not attempting to say that all well-meaning people involved in the international anti-apartheid movement have developed a vested interest in the struggle. The point is well made, however, throughout the article, that very often the small coterie of those in control are making decisions and statements and applying pressures which are not helping democratic processes to develop.

There is a tendency withn South Africa and abroad to constantly denigrate changes in this country and to act as though they were meaningless. Of course the complete destruction of apartheid and our eventual liberation are our ultimate objectives but what people so often forget is that the very changes happening on the ground now were more often than not brought about by the sweat and the dogged determination of the black masses.

They need encouragement as they burrow further into the bastions of apartheid; the Government too should be encouraged as they reluctantly give way to black demands which will eventually lead to negotiations.

That change is not happening fast enough is true enough, but it is taking place. When those in the anti-apartheid movement abroad and others constantly act as though no reforms have been constructive, as though we have stood still for decades, they discredit the very people they purport to support because nothing would have happened at all if it hadn't been for black South Africans creating the climate for those reforms.

Is it the fact that blacks and a growing number of whites in South Africa are instigating change peacefully that irks those with power in the international anti-apartheid movement? Do they really believe that the slow and painful negotiating process to come can be negated and that, overnight, by some miracle, there will be a new and democratic government in South Africa brought about by the masses? Or, are they hanging in there with a defined agenda determined to create circumstances in which they and those they represent will eventually dictate change; that they will author who the players will be? Doesn't this smack of revolutionary and undemocratic minds at work?

These are the people who dictate through their powerful networks which black and white South African musicians, playwrights, authors, sportsmen, academics and others are acceptable to work or participate in programmes abroad. These are the people who attempt to block academic, cultural, sports and other exchanges to South Africa.

They give the nod to those who should, in their minds, be given platforms and refuse those who they think should not. These people operate from democratic societies and yet decide unilaterally that all black South Africans want to suffer through the implementation of sanctions. They themselves will never have to witness the resulting horrors of their actions. Many support violent protest and applaud and join hands with those who kill for political gain. These are just a few examples of their tactics as they beat their chests against the injustices of tyranny when they themselves have turned intimidation and denial of human rights into an art form!

It is now time for the broad mass of anti-apartheid supporters abroad to think again about their actions. Peace-lovers, deeply affected by black suffering, have inadvertently or otherwise begun supporting revolutionaries they would term terrorists anywhere else in the world.

Americans and Europeans and citizens of other countries have begun evolving double standards by praising actions in and against South Africa that they would totally condemn in any civilised country in the West.

South Africa has all the makings of a totally destructive civil war and I urgently call on leaders, individuals, organisations, pressure groups within Governments and others in the West to stop playing political parlour games around Western perceptions and interests and to stop dabbling with the fate of apartheid's victims.

However portentous circumstances are now becoming for real breakthroughs in the drive to establish a non-racial, multi-party democracy in South Africa, the battle is certainly not already won and I know the going will be tough. This is always the case in the politics of transition. Times of transition are times of danger.

Those who can assist in the transition must get in and do what needs to be done, and those who cannot offer assistance in making the transition to the future through non-violent means in the politics of negotiation must get out. The fight against apartheid is not a party political affair. It is radical changes in institutionalised South Africa that are required. Those who are hampering this institutional adjustment to a post-apartheid society must remove themselves.

Those in the international community who do not believe that we are in these crucial times and that we can now make the breakthroughs the whole Western world is waiting for must be shunted aside by those who do believe it. We cannot have a twin stream of Western influences, one working for the politics of negotiation and one working on the assumption that the politics of negotiation cannot yet take place and that harsh measures are needed to soften up the South African Government.

To act on claimed knowledge of what black South Africans want is immoral. The issues are so crucial that actions should be taken only on proof of what blacks really want and not just on the rhetorical simplicities of some who purport to speak on our behalf. Black South Africans have said 'no' many millions of times to sanctions and disinvestment. They have said 'yes' to peaceful change, negotiation and maximisation of the country's growth rate. They have clearly not supported to any significant degree whatsoever, bloodshed and an armed struggle.

The war of words internationally against leaders who reject confrontation and punitive sanctions (British Prime Minister Mrs Margaret Thatcher is an example) is terribly damaging. Things are finely balanced in South Africa at this stage and it is we in this country, dominantly the poorest of the poor, who pay prices for Western blundering.

Western analysts must reject anything which might fail and which might have a cost which only we will pay. It is utterly wrong, both morally and politically, for the West to undertake action for which it cannot pay the price of failure. That gives the West the luxury to be adventurist in politics. We cannot afford political adventurism. We are moving away from political adventurism in South Africa. We are gravitating towards the politics of greater sanity and we are doing this because we are paying prices for failures to eradicate apartheid which are totally unacceptable.

I can do no more than stress with every fibre of my being that the kind of national unity achieved after apartheid will depend on the degree of unity achieved in the process of eradicating it.

When I write of civil war, the harsh reality is that South Africa has a highly militarised white community which will make the best of what Renamo could do in Mozambique and Unita in Angola look rather amateurish. White revolutionaries will have immense advantages which their black counterparts never had in Mozambique and Angola. They have technology; they will be ensconced in crucial positions and they have a vast mobility that was never there for Mozambicans and Angolans.

Any attempt to eradicate apartheid by violent means, or even through the kind of confrontationist tactics which further alienates black and white, will be fatal for us. We need now to bridge gaps; we need now to de-escalate conflict; we need now to seek common cause and we need to work towards the accommodation of that which is ineradicably present in every race group. It is no use thinking idealistically about what people ought to do. As a politician and as a leader, I must deal with what people *are* doing.

My leadership has consequences for people and at all times I must ensure that they are consequences the people are asking for. What the West does has consequences for black South Africans, as well as for the white South African Government against which the West is acting.

There is in the West a kind of dangerous romanticism about freedom fighters and there is also a sympathy for the politics of violent protest in South Africa. Centre field forces, which must ultimately salvage our country from the ruins of apartheid and stave off the threats of destructive violence, are devalued by this romanticism and misplaced sympathy.

Not only those black South Africans who have elected to take up arms are angry. It is my contention that anger is a national asset which must be employed and not squandered.

One sees evidence of this every day as black South Africans, angry that they have been forced to live in black townships, move quietly into so-called white areas. Job reservation and the Pass Laws made blacks angry and so they challenged these laws and ultimately defeated them. Inferior education has made angry blacks determined to succeed and attend universities which used to be reserved for whites only. All this is evidence of anger used constructively; anger that has built something worthwhile out of adversity.

To my mind it is imperative that the majority of black South Africans continue to strive for noble ends and central to this, as I have stressed, is their right to choose their own leaders and how they want to be led.

There is no society in the world where the kind of violence now being employed in South Africa – by the State and by a divided black opposition – will produce an open, democratic society. Political victories which have as their aftermath mass poverty and disunity and which have destroyed the means of production, result in post-victory governments attempting to govern what is ultimately ungovernable.

If we do not achieve national reconciliation in the process of liberating South Africa, and if liberation does not result in national reconciliation, we will not be able to make the national effort to reconstruct South African society that millions of young South Africans now demand we do.

It is simply pernicious to argue, as some do, that democratic opposition to apartheid has failed and there is only violence left. In pure logic, violent opposition has failed just as much as democratic opposition has. It is just as tenable to argue that violence must now be abandoned after the attempt over more than a quarter of a century to use it to bring about change. What visible evidence is there that the South African Government is about to be toppled by revolutionary violence?

What will make a revolution work in South Africa? I have often listed three main ingredients – none of which apply to this country.

(1) Revolutionary forces have to have a 'liberated zone' within the country which can act as a springboard for attacks against the State, or at least a springboard in an adjacent state from which attacks can be mounted.

Revolutionaries in South Africa and across our borders have neither and their position is worsening by the day as Frontline State leaders call for negotiation and, in reality, can no longer afford to support exiled groups within their countries.

(2) The security forces and the civil service must be divided in their loyalty to the Government. There is no evidence that the S.A. police, army or civil service harbour revolutionary threats.

(3) The masses in South Africa have to support revolutionary activity in sympathetic daily practice.

This is not the case. The majority of black South Africans, when affected by pro-violence forces, have to be intimidated into destructive activity and support for it by hideous means.

Since some adopted the armed struggle as the primary means of liberating South Africa, divisions in the black body politic have grown and blacks have been the victims of black violence in many forms.

My colleague, Dr Oscar Dhlomo, speaking at a conference in the United States of America some years ago, expressed my viewpoint in this way: 'The real problem in black politics today is disunity, which has lowered the level of political debate to a mudslinging diatribe among organisations that should be co-operating to achieve the broad aim of black liberation.

'The blind pursuit of ideological purity, the failure to communi- cate and co-operate seen among groups that pursue alternative liberatory strategies, and the inability to perceive the S.A. struggle as a multi-dimensional one – all these are responsible for fragment- ing the liberation struggle in South Africa.'

The dismantling of apartheid by and of itself would not necessarily lead to a new and democratic South Africa overnight.

The policy of apartheid has permeated virtually all aspects of

South African life and Dr Dhlomo noted that 'people who will genuinely be considered to have taken a giant leap forward in the democratisation of South Africa are those who will help us find a lasting solution to the problem of black disunity in our country.'

This is what we are asking the West to help us do while seriously contemplating their own actions.

When one looks at what has to be done for black to find black and black to find white and vice versa across the political barriers that now divide us, I believe that there are two different directions in which we have to work.

The first direction is to define what common ground already exists between us. When we know what we believe together, when we know what we want together and we have defined the common ground which I know is there binding us together as sons and daughters of Africa, then we can start looking at what differences there are that could be, but should not be, separating us.

I hear the bells tolling for black South Africa. I hear the call of history and I know that unless we now rise to be one people, there will not be the one South Africa with one sovereign Parliament for all that we and our forefathers have always striven for.

The first thing we have as we define our common bonds is our citizenship of South Africa. It is a citizenship granted to us by history under the guiding hand of the Almighty. The citizenship of the land of our birth is ours by divine decree. No man dare take it away from us and no man will succeed in doing so.

We as blacks *will* achieve the full citizenship of South Africa that is our right. All black South Africans who struggle to establish South Africa as one sovereign place in which there will be one Parliament are brothers in the struggle.

You can walk across South Africa from border to border and wherever you stop to speak to black people, you will find that they believe that they are not only the sons and daughters of Africa, the citizens of South Africa, but you will find that they believe they should have the vote. The ideals of one South Africa with one sovereign Parliament, resting on one universal adult franchise system, is there in the heart and mind of every black South African.

The unity that we should be experiencing and the realisation of this fundamental truth of there being one South Africa and one people in it joined to each other by divine decree, defines many problems.

When we as a black people have seen how hideous the

consequences are of a government putting the good of the Party before the good of the State, or the good of the minority before the good of the majority, we just dare not ourselves follow suit.

Tragically, though, the good of the Party is for some blacks more important than the good of the State. And the good of their minority around that Party is for them above the good of the majority.

In Inkatha and KwaZulu, we will not be intimidated out of our claim to be part of a majority which will in the end decide the destiny of South Africa. We demand the right to work to form majority opinions and to work within the majority opinion once it is formed. We reject politics based on racial discrimination. We reject ethnicity as the building blocks of constitutions.

There is one South Africa; there is one body politic; there shall be one Parliament and it shall be guided by one majority. No amount of denial of our fundamental human rights by the State will drive us to accept anything less. I say the same for any other form of oppressive opposition. We will not be battered out of our grasping the great gifts of God. We will not be intimidated into accepting that others can dictate to us what should happen and that others can spurn the majority of the people. Above all, we demand the right to establish the democratic machinery through which majority opinion can eventually emerge.

Once we have the basic commitments to pursue democratic ideals, I believe we can then turn our attention to what form of democracy would best survive in South Africa. I place the emphasis on survival of democracy. It is no use my, or anybody else, wanting a form of democracy that will not survive. Democracy must spell out constitutional stability and it must spell out personal group stability. This again is something which should unify black South Africa.

When we have the mechanisms of democracy we will be better able to protect the minority rights of whites, Indians or Coloureds. Without democracy there is no protection for anybody. I am quite adamant that we cannot rediscover the wheels of democracy. We know what democracy means in everyday language. We know what it means in constitutional terms and we demand nothing other.

There is simply no need for any black-on-black confrontation over fundamental issues in South Africa. They are not there amongst the people. They are not found at the grass root level.

Differences which result in violent confrontations and which divide black from black are imposed on the majority of the people by working minorities of one kind or another.

The more we do to define what we have in common, the more we will be able to define our differences out of existence. It is when we have enough in common that we can meet in common purpose to find the best way of achieving what we all want.

If we are to reach out to find each other at this critical point in our South African history, we must both define what we have in common and discuss alternatives in tactics and strategies and alternatives in goals within the realisation that anything that is destructive of the common cause we have as South Africans is unpatriotic and must be rejected.

I believe that all that I have said in pleading for black unity in South Africa, and all that I believe we should be striving for, was eloquently put forward in a message by Pope John Paul II in a statement for a World Day for Social Communications several years ago: 'Peace is not possible without dialogue . . . From the balance of apprehension, to that of fear and finally to that of terror, springs a cold peace. Only communication can, through dialogue, bring about a desire and expectancy of warm peace . . . Every war can lose everything, and nothing can be lost with peace.'

Apartheid is in a coma – what will negotiations bring? **6**

We must either learn to live together as brothers or we shall perish together as fools.

Dr Martin Luther King.

When looking at constitutional models and other associated proposals for a future non-racial post-apartheid South Africa, I cannot afford to be prescriptive. I have always said that I will support anything that is genuinely acceptable to the majority that will really work. I do not believe that democracy *à la* Westminster was ordained by God, even though I have desired it all my adult life. There are many democratic constitutional examples in the free world that we can look to and adapt for our own particular purposes.

My overall feeling is that we might eventually end up with one or another form of federal government. However, if white South Africans want to succeed in establishing something like this and move away from a one-man-one-vote system of government in a unitary state, there will have to be a lot more give and take than the ruling National Party now seems prepared for.

There is no great, grand, evil force in life stopping the people of South Africa from authoring a beautiful future for their country and for future generations. If there is no future it will be because what we do authors that fact.

Inkatha is emphatically a black political organisation which seeks to establish a multi-party democracy. It is our point of view that the people themselves – black and white – have the sole right to author the destiny of South Africa. Those refinements of democracy which distinguish one political party from another in the free world are hopefully refinements we will have one day in South Africa. Right now, the basic freedom of choice is what we struggle for.

South Africa, first of all, needs to establish a government which governs by consensus and in such a way that all the people of this country accept the way in which they are governed. In so many ways I keep saying that political victories are meaningless unless they lead to the evolution of a national will to survive, and Africa has taught me that political victories against oppression that leave behind a polarised society are empty victories for the people.

I have to constantly bear in mind how dangerous it is to borrow revolutionary models from elsewhere as though there is a one-to-one fit between the circumstances in which they would have to succeed elsewhere and the circumstances in which they would have to succeed in South Africa. I am constantly aware that revolutionary organisations in our context could form a dangerous elite which inevitably predisposes them to establishing one-party states in which they are the sole authority.

The historically proved systems and the tried-and-tested solutions adopted in working democracies will guide me in what I am prepared to accept and what I am prepared to compromise upon.

The politics of transition in which we now find ourselves hold difficulties for all political groupings in South Africa. Inkatha and the KwaZulu Government are therefore committed to be allies of any group seeking an open race-free democracy in South Africa based on one sovereign parliament resting on universal adult suffrage.

We are now in a position in which we really can and should be devoting attention to the consequences of political tactics for human relationships. We in Inkatha, then, go further in reiterating our willingness to negotiate individual and group right protection within the framework of a future race-free democracy and call on other black groups to offer white South Africa safe custody through the transitionary period which lies ahead.

The ruling National Party Government says it is committed to a new constitution for the country, to negotiations with black leaders, and a five-year plan of action for a new South Africa, which I feel is relevant to detail.

What we are looking at here is the National Party's starting point in the process of negotiations. I have always argued that the ruling

National Party will have to have a role in negotiating radical change in South Africa if change is going to come about through peaceful means. Any national negotiations about the constitutional future of South Africa will have to give a central place to the South African Government.

I carry no bags for the National Party and I will carry no bags for it even if it sets about getting the politics of negotiation on track. I am in business to oppose the State President, Mr F. W. de Klerk, and the National Party and I will oppose them for as long as racist measures remain on the Statute Books.

I am intensely aware that the National Party will drive for, bargain for, and if necessary fight for, a new South Africa in which whites contain the kind of political whip-hand which enables the dominating white political party to be the final authors of domestic and foreign policy. It is for this reason that I authored the draft Declaration of Intent outlined in a previous chapter which I said was the kind of declaration both black and white leaders must subscribe to before meaningful negotiations about the constitutional future of South Africa can get off the ground.

The process of negotiations to come, I repeat, is going to be tough and compromises will have to be made. For black South Africa our land is one country and only one sovereign parliament resting on universal adult franchise will be acceptable to the majority. Democracies in various parts of the world do protect minority rights but the notion of South Africa being a country of minorities within the context of white claims to have sovereign rights as a white minority in 87 per cent of the land is totally absurd.

The ruling National Party says it envisages that South Africa must be a democracy in which:

☐ No group dominates or is dominated;
☐ The independence of the judiciary is upheld and honoured;
☐ Civilised norms apply;
☐ A dynamic economy thrives, based on free enterprise;
☐ Everybody lives in safety and harmony; and
☐ In good neighbourly relationship with the international community.

Its plan of action calls for Parliament to instruct a body of credible and independent experts to study all possible constitutional models, and to define the implications, advantages and disadvantages of each model.

A report should then be tabled in Parliament and deal with

(1) The constitutional options available to prevent domination of one group by another;

(2) The methods by which a constitutional dispensation may effectively protect the political rights and values of groups and the practical implications of the various models and

(3) Methods available to entrench such a constitution against future amendment or repeal which may result in the infringement of individual and group rights.

The crux of Government thinking at the moment is obviously based on its obsession with group rights, and the National Party spells this out quite clearly in its 'key objectives' which it says it plans to follow in the five years following its September 1989 white general election victory.

These are:

□ To promote a set of common values as a basis for a peaceful political system, without inhibiting the identity of groups;

□ To engage recognised leaders of all groups committed to the pursuit of peaceful solutions in talks and negotiations about the political, social and economic systems for a new South Africa;

□ To make a definite start, based on these discussions and negotiations, with the setting up of institutions in which the leaders of all groups can participate in the creation of a new system;

□ To re-assess the functions and powers of the head of state in a new system, his role or otherwise as head of government, and the manner in which he should be elected.

The Government says its plan is that 'every South African has the right to participate in political decision-making on all levels of government which affect his interests, subject to the principle of no domination . . .' Separate identities should not be 'ignored, prejudiced or undermined' and in a section headed 'No Domination: Group Protection' the plan states the following:

'The South African population consists of a variety of groups that evolved as a result of cultural and historical factors. This can easily lead to a power struggle and to domination, dictatorship and tyranny, as has often happened elsewhere. To avoid this, the diversity of groups must be fully taken into account in a new South Africa of the future.'

It seems clear that the Government is trying to create a public image of attempting to get away from the concept of race groups as a criterion and convince white South Africa that there must be a shift to culturally defined groups.

This is reinforced in the document under a heading 'Self-Determination' which says, in part: 'In a state where cultures and interests differ, it is extremely important to extend this federal principle (of area, regional and through group governments) so that each area or population group has as much say as possible about its own affairs. This is another building block in the process of protecting the rights of minorities and preventing domination.

'Consequently the principle of self-determination regarding own affairs, along with the principle of power-sharing regarding general affairs, should be sensibly developed through the division and the devolution of the power of the central government to regional, area or group governments and local authorities where the need is felt . . .'

I can only look at this plan with interest and ask: Is this apartheid in a different guise? There is no way I can endorse it in its present form. What is important is that we have a commitment to negotiations, whatever they may be initially, and quite clearly they will have to bridge vast differences which exist between parties and between race groups. This will not happen overnight.

There is now at least a small ray of hope that the National Party can move towards one or another form of democracy which the Western industrial world will recognise as a democracy and which Africa will endorse as moving in the right direction.

Negotiation will have to be about fundamental constitutional issues and right now the National Party is talking too much about detail and thinking too little about basic principles. There is a black majority in South Africa which will find political expression as a majority. That is totally inevitable.

Now is the time for cool heads all round. Mistakes could be made in black and white politics which could cost everyone very dearly.

We need to separate where we are going from how we are going to get there. The National Party needs now to say more about its preparedness to totally scrap the present tricameral parliamentary system and show its willingness to move towards a new democracy in which there is total equality before the law and the constitution.

Black South Africa wants to see the Government scrap the Population Registration Act, the Group Areas Act and other backbones of apartheid legislation. Once the Government has put its own political camp in order only then can it look to making a joint declaration with black leaders about the ultimate purpose of negotiations. Until then, the National Party will have nobody coming forward worth negotiating with.

I have told Mr de Klerk, in public statements, that if I were in his shoes I would concentrate on making sure that the people who ought to be negotiating are persuaded to negotiate. The future will judge him on whether he can do this.

A great many blacks agree with Mr de Klerk that we must get on with the job of negotiating and stop all petty politicking. Negotiations are only possible, however, if black democracy is unshackled and if the South African Government does not think that it will be able to continue sitting in the driving seat. For me to even think about being involved in negotiations, Mr de Klerk is going to have to pronounce the death sentence on the present constitution.

After the September 1989 tricameral parliamentary election in which the National Party lost votes to the left and to the right, I issued a statement which said I saw the results as an event heralding what should be an entirely new and very distinctive political era.

Even though the National Party now has fewer seats (93) than it has ever had since the 1950s, my view is that it has now emerged stronger than it has ever been before because it is now no longer trammelled with ultra-conservatism among its rank and file members. It is a party purged of the right wing brake on reform progress. Furthermore, while the right wing Conservative Party has now peaked, the Democratic Party to the left of the National Party is now at the bottom of what could well be a steep growth curve to come, having captured 33 seats in the election.

For me politically this all means that the National Party has beaten the Conservative Party at the polls and it will now have to look over its left shoulder and not its right shoulder.

The time has come for black leaders to be bold. The National Party's victory, following as it does the Party's rejection of the old-style former State President P. W. Botha's leadership, and the old-style P. W. Botha objectives, must provide us all with more flexibility which will make a greater range of initiatives possible. The test of our own black political skills will come in the form of how best we can employ black political bargaining power and black political advantage and lead Mr de Klerk away from the rest of the National Party's failing policies.

I don't say this in some kind of starry-eyed innocence. I am aware that whether or not the positiveness of my thoughts turn out to be justified depends both upon Mr de Klerk having the guts to go further than he ever thought he would have to go, and black politics having the guts to encourage him when he does go in the right direction. That we are in a new era cannot now be doubted. I pause only to remember what classical Verwoerdian apartheid was and to perceive that the Conservative Party, which supports what can only be termed as Verwoerdian party politics, now holds 39 out of 166 seats. This shows the extent to which the National Party has been forced away from its earlier dreams.

If Mr de Klerk does not prove man enough for the job ahead of him, history will trample on him and the future fight will be for somebody who can walk with history, whether it is a State President chosen by the National Party in interim politics or whether it is a State President chosen by the Democratic Party in interim politics.

South Africa is now moving towards the achievement of democracy and the politics of negotiation and no National Party leader in the history of this country has been more favourably placed to take bold steps than Mr de Klerk.

History has done no more than present South Africa with an epoch-making golden opportunity. It is history that is giving the whole of the country a chance, not just the National Party. We can of course spurn the opportunity but as I see it history demands a multi-racial response to this chance to move South Africa into a race-free democracy.

The Government is going to have to respond to the demand for the normalisation of South Africa which came across loud and clear in the election results. It won't be able to move forward without getting black support for what it intends doing.

Mr de Klerk must now move away from his preoccupation with group politics and I believe that blacks must encourage him if he is genuine about negotiations, and not make it impossible for him to rise above the traditional constraints which have always operated in the National Party. This is why we in Inkatha and KwaZulu were prepared to co-operate in a joint S.A. Government/KwaZulu committee investigating obstacles impeding negotiations in South Africa.

It is important, I think, to quote in full the working document of the KwaZulu delegation which it presented to this committee.

Working document of the KwaZulu Government presented to the joint South African/KwaZulu committee investigating obstacles impeding negotiations in South Africa

A. Preamble
It is accepted that there are real obstacles impeding negotiations in South Africa and that unless these obstacles are clearly identified and sincerely addressed negotiation politics will not take off.

B. Obstacles as identified by the KwaZulu Delegation
1. Exclusive as opposed to inclusive negotiations
The South African Government seems to favour exclusive negotiations (i.e. negotiations that exclude certain groups and individuals who, for one reason or the other, are not acceptable to the Government as negotiating partners). The KwaZulu Government favours inclusive negotiations (i.e. negotiations that include all groups and individuals without any pre-conditions). KwaZulu believes that inclusive negotiations would entail the acceptance of the following measures by the South African Government:

1.1 The immediate and unconditional release of Mr Nelson Mandela and other Rivonia Trialists as well as the release of all those political prisoners that have already served sentences of over 15 years. Other political prisoners must also be considered for release.
1.2 Declaration of an amnesty which would enable all political exiles to return to South Africa and participate in negotiations. The amnesty would have to be adequately guaranteed and returning exiles would need to be assured of immunity from prosecution.
1.3 Unbanning of organisations so that the leaders might freely consult with their followers before and during negotiations.
1.4 The lifting of the State of Emergency, the release of political detainees and the restoration of press freedom. This should be done to facilitate free debate and assembly.

2. Removal of Discriminatory Laws. It is accepted that all discriminatory laws cannot be removed overnight in South Africa. Nevertheless there are specific laws that are regarded by the majority as 'pillars of apartheid'. The following laws would need to be removed before the start of negotiations:

2.1 The Group Areas Act
2.2 The Population Registration Act
2.3 The Separate Amenities Act

3. Inability of the Government To Allow Groups To Form Themselves Voluntarily And The Insistence That Only Race-Based Groups Should Be Constitutionally Recognised:
This inability is demonstrated by the Government's refusal to discuss any other alternative suggested formulae that seek to move away from rigid race classification, e.g. KwaZulu-Natal Indaba, geographic (as opposed to ethnic) federalism, etc., as well as the Government's inflexible belief that the only solution is rigid ethnic separation, e.g. the Homelands Policy and the tricameral parliamentary system.

4. The Existence Of the Tricameral Parliament:
One single obstacle to negotiations is the existence of the tricameral parliament (with all its consequences like the Regional Service Councils, Own Affairs, etc.) which are perceived by the black majority as entrenching apartheid and racism and making a mockery of the concept of power sharing.

C. *Procedures in addressing the obstacles*
1. Exclusive As Opposed To Inclusive Negotiations
Political Prisoners:
The following procedure should be adopted.
1.1 Mr Nelson Mandela And Other Rivonia Trialists
These should be released immediately and unconditionally.
1.2 Political Prisoners That Have Served Over Fifteen (15) Years
These should also be released immediately and unconditionally.
1.3 Other Political Prisoners
The principles of remission of sentence and parole should be immediately applied to all political prisoners that qualify as happens with other categories of prisoners.

2. Declaration Of An Amnesty:
2.1 The Government should announce an amnesty through appropriate national and international channels.
2.2 The co-operation of instances like the International Red Cross, the UN Commission For Refugees, Western Governments and the International Commission of Jurists should be sought encouraging exiles and refugees to take advantage of the amnesty.

3. Unbanning Of Organisations

Once prisoners under C1.1 and 1.2 are released, the Government should immediately negotiate with them the modalities for the unbanning of their organisations.

4. The Ending Of The State Of Emergency, The Release of Detainees And The Restoration Of Press Freedom:

The release of detainees and the restoration of press freedom should happen immediately and the lifting of the State of Emergency could be done either immediately or progressively according to districts and in accordance with a predetermined timetable before the start of negotiations. In any event C1, 2 and 3 would of necessity have to lead to the lifting of the State of Emergency, the release of detainees, and the restoration of press freedom.

5. Discriminatory Laws:

5.1 There are laws that are already being considered for abolition and these should be abolished immediately before negotiations begin, e.g. Group Areas Act, Separate Amenities Act and the Population Registration Act.

5.2 Other laws like the Land Acts of 1913 could then be phased out in accordance with a definite timetable which would be subject to negotiation.

6. Race-Based Group Concept:

6.1 The Government must announce its acceptance of the principle of voluntary association or freedom of association.

6.2 Voluntary groups that arise should enjoy protection from the State and their constitutional rights should be guaranteed.

7. Tricameral Parliament:

A mutually acceptable Statement of Intent should be issued stating clearly that negotiations would aim at replacing the tricameral system with a system acceptable to the majority of the people of South Africa.

D. *Points of common agreement*

1. Establishment of a united South Africa with one sovereign parliament:

If this principle is mutually acceptable then the qualification should be that no self-governing territory should henceforth be allowed to declare itself independent, and that the TBCV states that wish to rejoin a United South Africa should be allowed to do so.

2. Belief in a democratic, non-racial and multi-party political system.

3. Belief in the protection of individual and minority rights.

4. Belief in freedom of association for individuals regardless of race.

5. Belief in the free-enterprise economic system with built-in mechanisms to create wealth, eliminate poverty and afford disadvantaged sections of the South African population maximum opportunity to fully participate and have a meaningful stake in the economy.

This was the first tabled document of its kind that I know of presented to white South Africa by black South Africans earnestly intent on attempting to get negotiations off the ground, stating quite clearly many of the impediments that will have to be addressed before they can. Other input is also being placed before the Government which simply cannot be ignored.

In early 1989 the findings of the Government's legal think-tank, the South African Law Commission, were released. Produced after more than two years' work, the commission's instructions were to investigate the feasibility of protecting group rights within a Bill of Rights regime. The report, which was requested by the Minister of Justice, Mr Kobie Coetsee, quite clearly boomeranged on the Government.

While it was reported that the Minister hoped that a human rights ideology could provide a front for perpetuating a political system founded on race, the Commission, under the chairmanship of Mr Justice Pierre Oliver, regarded the perpetuation of apartheid in any form as being incompatible with the idea of human rights. Group rights could only be adequately protected through the entrenchment of individual rights.

The Law Commission came out boldly in a 500-page report which suggested that the introduction of a Bill of Rights should be linked to a new constitution and universal franchise.

The document stated: 'The present constitutional deadlock on the black vote will have to be resolved to the satisfaction of all if the Bill of Rights is to have credibility, for the simple reason that the right to vote is one of the fundamental human rights that must be enshrined in any constitution.'

The report recommended that discriminatory legislation should be abolished and that a 'limited version' of a Bill of Rights should be introduced immediately.

It stated that such a document would need to be approved by Parliament as well as 'the entire nation, regardless of race and colour.' It suggested a referendum be held.

The Commission said that no matter who governs South Africa, 'it goes without saying that if we are to avoid dictatorship – even the dictatorship of the democratic majority – we need such a Bill.'

It added: 'Too long has there been no concerted conscious action on the part of the State to put human rights first and to protect them, with the result that in our society insensitivity to those rights has taken root.'

In adopting a Bill of Rights 'the resultant image of justice and respect for the dignity of man that would thereby be promoted would invalidate many of the arguments of our critics . . .

'The courts are severely hampered as regards the protection of individual and group rights in the face of legislation which curtails these rights . . .'

The report, recommending that everyone over the age of 18 should have a vote, noted: 'It must be laid down that the constitution shall provide for the composition of the parliament within which equal and equivalent franchise can be realised.'

What the Commission was telling the Government was to get on with setting up a representative body to draft a new constitution for South Africa that would include a Bill of Rights.

Hailed by South African lawyers and many others as bold and forthright, and a remarkable, deeply impressive document, to date the Government appears to have put the totality of its findings on a back-burner – too hot to handle.

It is important to chronicle how liberal commentators of the South African situation read this, as they articulate the thinking of a growing number of white South Africans, and for this reason I quote their remarks at length. Their erudition is evidence of what I have always claimed: white South Africa is not beyond redemption and there is an emerging body of white South Africans who want to see positive, democratic change.

Once again I turn to the Editor of *Business Day*, Mr Ken Owen, who noted the following in an article on July 3, 1989 headlined *The five-year plan sets the stage for ten years' turmoil*: 'After 40 years of messianic self-certainty, the National Party is at last beginning to struggle honestly, I think, with the central issue of South African politics, which is liberty. It fails because it cannot break out of the South African paradigm: the obsession with groups.

'That is why the party leaders, in setting out their five-year plan last week, went to quite unusual lengths to suppress, or even to distort, the findings of the Law Commission on the need for a South African Bill of Rights.

'The problem is that the party's plan of action flies in the face of the central findings of the Law Commission: that rights vest in the individual, not the group. And the Nationalists remain wedded to "the white group", which is neither culturally coherent, nor linguistically uniform, nor politically united, nor even very religious.

'The Law Commission's Working Paper 25, drawn up under the chairmanship of Mr Justice Pierre Olivier, a Government-appointed Free Stater, puts forward its own plan, conservative but workable, to take South Africa to democracy. The differences between the NP plan and the Law Commission's plan are illuminating.

'The Law Commission calls, first of all, for a statement of policy by Parliament "that it is in favour of the protection, in a Bill of Rights, of the generally accepted individual rights and cultural, religious and linguistic values."

'Then, it suggests, Government should embark immediately on the major task of systematically repealing all laws which would conflict with the Bill of Rights. The effect of this process, of course, would be steadily to widen the area of liberty for those South Africans most deprived of it.

'Simultaneously, says the Law Commission, there must be a thorough process of education on questions of human rights, followed by negotiations on a new constitution, which should be submitted finally to referendum.

'The test of this plan, as of the NP's five-year plan, is not whether it meets some intellectual or moral criterion, but whether it will bring the country to rest. Since it carries the promise of democracy – of equality before the law, liberty and justice – at the end of it, the Law Commission's plan has a chance of success. Probably nothing less can succeed.

'The chances of its success lie in the content which it gives to a Bill of Rights – rights which no legislation would be permitted to infringe . . .

'The Law Commission distinguishes between political rights,

intended to protect minorities against oppression, and other rights. The former, it says, are matters for negotiation, to be incorporated in an agreed constitution; the latter must be protected by the Bill of Rights, as belonging to the individual.

'Its words on this point are worth quoting exactly: "In our society, cultural, religious and linguistic values should not be protected as 'group rights' since a group is not a legal persona. These rights should be protected in a Bill of Rights by way of individual rights."

'"In public law," the commission says at one point, "our courts have never recognised an entity known as a 'group' or a 'minority' which can, as such, enforce rights."

'Elsewhere it says: "It is unnecessary to protect the so-called group interests or minority interests in the sphere of culture, religion or language by trying to define the group concerned and conferring legal personality upon it. All that is needed is to designate the interests in question as interests protected by law and to leave it to any individual to protect the interests through court proceedings where necessary."

'This approach – if only the National Party would realise it – takes care of all the legitimate concerns of minorities. Indeed, the Commission is emphatic: "The protection of minorities in this country is essential, since to ignore the rights of minority groups would be to invite endless conflict."

'Even the right to dissociate, so beloved of National Party politicians, is catered for, subject to the all-important qualification that it will not include practising discrimination on the ground of race, colour, religion, language, or culture if public funds are used. Exclusive groups, whether churches or clubs, wine-tasters or garlic-eaters, will be permitted provided they pay for their own exclusivity.

'With these ideas before them, the National Party have opted instead to search for a constitutional model "to prevent domination of one group by another." Instead of accepting the Bill of Rights, put forward by the Law Commission, the NP talks of "considering the advisability" of a Bill of Rights . . .

'The five-year plan talks of representation, but no equal representation; of rights, but not of equality. The party still hovers at the edge of democracy, not daring to plunge . . .

'But there is no middle ground. All discussion of democracy begins, it does not end, with universal franchise. The National

Party, under a new leader, had the chance to commit itself to a democratic system, to adopt the ten-year plan of the Law Commission and to create a prospect of peace in the 1990s. Instead, it has chosen to continue the vain search for the elusive formula to preserve racism by another name.

'By that choice, it has built conflict and turmoil into the next decade.' (*Business Day*, July 3, 1989).

As a black leader who has the most to gain by the politics of negotiation getting off the ground and the most to lose by failing negotiations, I will be positive wherever it is possible to be positive.

When one looks at, for instance, the work of the South African Law Commission and other dynamics I have mentioned previously, one must recognise that there is an internal South African democratic process at work which is obscured for the most part nationally and internationally.

The Government's so-called 'reform' process has not failed to get off the ground because reform is impossible in South Africa. South Africa is in a melting pot and the National Party is there in that same pot together with black political organisations which have their own agendas.

If the National Party now appears to be failing to mount an effective reform programme and if black democratic non-violent opposition to apartheid has not yet produced a winning thrust, then so have revolutionary forces failed to bring about change.

Politics in South Africa now is going to sort out the men from the boys. The weak are going to be crushed and the inept sidelined. Those who emerge as viable leaders with real constituencies will not be the kind of leaders who will be drawn into constitutional philandering. Real constituency leaders in South Africa will be the major actors who know where political survival and where political doom lie.

In a very real sense the South African Government now knows that its reform programme, or any elaborations of it, are completely at the mercy of black participation. When the reform programmes Mr de Klerk pursues are minimally correct, he will have minimal black participation. When they are wrong, he will have wrong black participation. Wrong agendas and inadequate vision will not be supported by black constituency leaders.

Radical change is now, as I have emphasised, totally inevitable in South Africa. Whether it comes about by revolutionary violence (which I sincerely doubt) or whether it comes through the politics of negotiation, there will be radical change.

The prime actors who will try to ensure that this change does take place are already there in the field. The political process must comprehend the interests and the inputs of these major actors. There will not be a new South Africa because new political forces emerge. There will be a new South Africa because existing political forces which dominate the political stage are there to make it happen.

The National Party is extremely vulnerable and we will see, as time goes on, that it is subject to all the stresses and strains of a Party in transition.

I think the time has come for blacks to risk entering the politics of negotiation under certain cirumstances because the State does not have the power to replace one version of apartheid with another version and to call the same thing by a different name. The politics of change can now best be ensured through the politics of negotiation and I believe real black powers in South Africa want non-violent tactics and strategies to succeed because this will be the quickest and the best way to succeed.

Social, economic and political forces are now building up in South Africa which are going to thrash apartheid without relying on those who are committed to war and revolution and ultimately socialism in a one-party state.

This does not mean, of course, that elements in the latter are going to give up without a fight. They are using every means at their disposal to perpetuate the myth that there can only be a two-sided negotiating table: The African National Congress and its allies on one side and the National Party and its allies on the other. Where does this leave Inkatha, the Pan African Congress (PAC), Black Consciousness organisations, the Democratic Party, the Conservative Party, various other black, Indian and Coloured political parties and movements and numerous interest groups already in existence, who will undoubtedly coalesce as additional political forces once negotiation really does become a reality?

As a wide spectrum of commentators note, the ANC is trying to force a single choice on South Africa: an ANC-led socialist state or apartheid. The National Party, it is said, responds with another message to the nation: a group-based constitution or the ANC's socialism.

An ANC document outlining guidelines for a negotiated

settlement in South Africa – adopted by the Organisation of African Unity special committee on Southern Africa in August 1989 – declared that:

'. . . Discussions should take place between the liberation movement and the South African regime to achieve the suspension of hostilities on both sides by agreeing to a mutually binding ceasefire . . .' What they mean by 'the liberation movement' is the ANC and its allies. Attempts by the OAU to get the ANC and the PAC to co-operate failed miserably. The ANC is attempting to be seen holding the negotiating high ground. Other organisations, to their mind, are irrelevant.

As I see it, the ANC is worried not only by the growing international climate of reconciliation but by the prospect of being outmanoeuvred or even excluded by the negotiation process (however inadequate now) being set in motion by the South African Government.

Both are under pressure from the West to commence negotiations and the ANC, which enjoys Soviet support, is getting a message from Moscow that a compromise political settlement may be necessary. Events are moving a little too fast for the ANC and the problem it now faces is that of being forced to respond to the SA Government rather than the reverse.

The ANC's strategy of mass insurrection has failed; the bombing campaign of its armed wing, Umkhonto we Sizwe, has failed. Its diplomatic initiative is all it has going for it. Now the organisation will have the problem of maintaining internal unity if it becomes involved in participating in peaceful negotiations where compromises will without doubt have to be made. It is one thing to negotiate with a defeated enemy, but quite another to do so with one which is not only very powerful but which is quietly supported by Western allies who would quite happily settle for a compromise solution.

Western support for the ANC is largely based on the SA Government's past refusal to have anything to do with it. Now the Government has been talking to its leader, Dr Nelson Mandela, and the Government has indicated a willingness to talk to the ANC.

The ANC has generally seen negotiations as an event from which power would be 'transferred to the people.' It desperately wants to secure for itself the role of sole negotiator and keep the upper hand – with everybody else having to sit on the side of the

S.A. Government – and this is quite clearly a recipe for disaster and political arrogance in the extreme.

Any negotiating process that is not all-embracing will fail. In the meantime we must expect that the ANC and its allies will do everything they can to eliminate and marginalise rival claimants to power and to heighten conflict within the country. These are not only my feelings.

This is why black democracy and black unity within South Africa must get on track now. I have never excluded the ANC from the role it should play, but it is imperative that black political forces, alongside white political forces, must actively make evident their part in ensuring that a multi-party free-enterprise democracy triumphs – with or without the co-operation of the ANC. It is their choice. The Government must, at the same time, eliminate conflict areas by repealing the State of Emergency, releasing and unbanning political prisoners and organisations and dismantling apartheid.

No organisation that cares about South Africa should sit back and cynically attempt to buy time for their own political advantage. South Africa and all its peoples are what really matter. Inkatha and the KwaZulu Government have shown at the regional level that blacks and whites can get together to thrash out compromise proposals for constitutional developments. Our attitude has been that while the Government continues to bungle about negotiation at the national level, it must stand alone while it does so. I have engaged the Government at the national level. I have also done so at the regional level.

We have become actively involved in regional planning which is attempting to look well into the future. In 1980 I established the Buthelezi Commission to look at alternatives to apartheid in the KwaZulu/Natal region of South Africa. After the Commission had submitted its report, I engaged with the then Natal Provincial Council in negotiations about the establishment of a Joint Black/White Executive Authority in the region. These negotiations eventually succeeded and there is now a Black/White Joint Executive Authority in KwaZulu/Natal. It is an operating non-racial reality. This Authority was established as a preliminary step towards negotiating a multi-racial Legislative Authority for the region.

The KwaZulu/Natal Indaba was brought into being as a result of a joint initiative of the KwaZulu Government and the Natal

Provincial Administration. In December 1987 it tabled its proposals for constitutional reform for the region. In essence the non-racial cross-section of participants produced, by consensus and compromise, a document recommending the region be established *within South Africa* as a united, non-racial democracy. A Bill of Rights forms a cornerstone of the Indaba's constitutional proposals.

The proposals have been laid before the Govenment and forces have been mobilised to oppose the Government's rejection of them. The Indaba's proposals for a multi-racial Joint Legislative Authority have created a situation of *realpolitik* in which these proposals are supported across race groups and across all traditional party political lines. Independent market research shows that the kind of proposals the Indaba has made are supported not only in centrist political forces but are also significantly supported by South Africans who claim allegiance to the ANC and the National Party.

Professor Marinus Weichers, a member of the constitutional committee and now the steering committee of the Indaba, who holds the Chair of Constitutional and International Law at the University of South Africa, wrote in a recent book *A Guide – South African Political Terms* (Tafelberg), that 'there is really no inspiration for political reconstruction other than aims of democracy.'

He added: 'Any other aim must necessarily lead to power demands, corruption, suppression, domination and a contamination of the process of reform. If there are nationally determined aims, political processes can be decentralised to the various corners of our country . . .'

In his vision of the future, the formation of parties must be promoted and not be placed under suspicion.

'Why should it not be possible to have a totally impartial body for constitutional negotiation and reconciliation, authorised to sponsor political parties with proven membership, democratic aims, party political life, effective leaders, and to support them with money and facilities?

'Regional plans which have gained acceptance through referenda must be implemented. This entire decentralised constitutional process and a constitutional creation of regional initiatives would be the foundation for the greater constitutional structure. In the end all these processes have to come together in a process of national constitution-making. The work of the political leaders, supported by their political followers and sealed in a referendum by the population as a whole, would finally be manifested in our national constitution.

'We are often told that a constitution for our country would have to be unique, something which the world has not yet seen, to make provision for our unique circumstances. This is not true. Our situation is very complex, but it is not so exceptional. In most countries in the world there are vast ethnic differences and minorities who need protection in a constitution. If we really wanted to follow a democratic path to reform, we would find that our future constitution bears all the marks and characteristics of many other constitutions . . . It is hoped that our future constitution will be so familiar that it will fit into the great democratic traditions . . .

'One of the conventional slogans of reform is that one can only negotiate and reform from a position of power. This becomes the destructive demand for more power – power to suppress, power to create violence, power to dominate. In truth the present is always the best time for negotiation and reform . . .'

Our involvement in the Indaba incurred the wrath of the ANC and its allies. We were accused of treachery and of attempting to fragment the struggle for liberation! All this and more when we honestly set out to show that a non-racial democracy was possible within South Africa and hopefully that our example, if permitted to operate, would take hold elsewhere and spread throughout the rest of the country. If this proliferation of democracy became a reality, quite obviously an entirely new constitutional dispensation for South Africa would be negotiated and put into practice.

The bottom line of our antagonists was that all should stand still until power is handed to the people. The question of non-participation has been discussed as a strategy in black politics for a very long time. It has now been elevated to a sacrosanct political principle.

It is interesting to see what ANC leader Dr Nelson Mandela wrote on participatory opposition as long ago as February 1958. An extract from his article *The Struggle Has Many Tactics* reads as follows:

'In the opinion of some people, participation in the system of separate racial representation in any shape or form, and irrespective of any reasons advanced for doing so, is impermissible on principle and harmful in practice. According to them such participation can only serve to confuse the people and foster the illusion that they can win their demands through a parliamentary form of struggle. In their view people have now become so politically conscious and developed that they cannot accept any form of representation which in any way fetters their progress. They maintain that people are demanding direct representation in parliament, in the provincial and city councils, and that nothing short of this will satisfy them. They say that leaders who talk of the practical advantages to be gained by participation in separate racial representation do not have the true interests of the people at heart. The basic error in this argument lies in the fact that it regards the boycott not as a tactical weapon to be employed if and when objective conditions permit but as an inflexible principle which must under no circumstances be varied.'

I became actively involved as a traditional and elected leader in KwaZulu because the people needed leadership to campaign against the Government's ideologies which proliferated after the National Party's electoral victory in 1948. I campaigned so vigorously against separate political institutions for KwaZulu that the complete rejection of these institutions by the Zulu people followed.

I set about opposing apartheid at the local, regional, provincial and national levels. I denounced apartheid and called for the rejection of the so-called homeland policy – a policy dividing black South Africa into ethnic groups with their own political identities and with their own political machinery – which separated them not only from white politics but from each other as well; a policy meant to denationalise black South Africans through 'independence' –so-called – by making them foreigners in 87 per cent of South Africa. We have successfully opposed this and protected the citizenship of not only Zulus but also that of millions of other blacks.

In its typical dictatorial fashion the Government then bluntly told us that we had no say in the matter and that they would be forced on us whether we liked it or not. This they proceeded to do and it was in these circumstances that I was asked to lead the Zulu people through the difficulties which lay ahead. I accepted the challenge to do so and in the situation which was imposed on us, assumed the role of Chief Executive Officer in the KwaZulu Territorial Authority, later Chief Executive Councillor and now Chief Minister. I vowed to lead my people in the tactics and strategies which would ensure that they would retain their South African citizenship and would continue to be entitled to exercise their democratic rights to oppose apartheid and any form of politics based on racial differentiation.

Until his tragic death I was encouraged by the President of the ANC, Chief Albert Lutuli, a Nobel Peace Prize recipient, who supported me as I campaigned among my people for the rejection of apartheid legislation. He clearly saw the threatened Balkanisation of South Africa as an impending catastrophe. Had those now in prominent roles in the ANC in exile paid more attention to the dangers which Chief Lutuli and I so clearly saw, and set out mobilising blacks in other areas as I mobilised them in KwaZulu, the South African Government would never have gone as far along the road as they did go to implement their homeland policy. Transkei, Bophuthatswana, Venda and Ciskei today would not be quasi so-called independent States.

KwaZulu has turned its back on so-called independence and the KwaZulu Government and Inkatha have become a bulwark of resistance against the Government. We have not been prepared to idly sit by and wait until our oppressors have been vanquished. The people have political expectations but they also have growing economic and social expectations and needs. We have had to get on with the job of serving them and trying to create advantages for them to assist them in improving their lot in life, however miserable the circumstances in which they find themselves.

When it comes to my participation in KwaZulu, those now in the ANC who reject me – pretending to do so because I occupy the position of Chief Minister – do so as part of their propaganda campaign. They know the truth. My only sin is that I refused to make Inkatha a surrogate of the ANC in exile. They are politically naive. Had I not accepted the challenge to lead in the way the people demanded, KwaZulu may well by now have been manipulated into the same positions as Transkei, Bophuthatswana, Venda and Ciskei.

I had a good relationship with Mr Oliver Tambo, President of the ANC, as Chief Minister of KwaZulu and President of Inkatha, until the abortive London meeting between him and ANC representatives and me and Inkatha Central Committee members in 1979. The ANC never made an issue of my position as Chief Minister of KwaZulu. This, after all, had been discussed with the leadership of the ANC prior to my accession to the chieftainship of the Buthelezi clan and prior to my assuming the position as First Advisor to King Cyprian Bhekuzulu ka Solomon and traditional 'Prime Minister' of the Zulu nation.

My only sin, as I have already stated, was that I could not agree that Inkatha be the internal wing of the ANC. I was prepared to co-operate with the ANC on those strategies we could synchronise. This was clearly not sufficient as far as ANC plans were concerned.

What we are doing in the KwaZulu/Natal region amounts to taking effective and realistic steps towards normalising South Africa as an industrialised democracy. There is vast support for the kind of things we are doing. South Africa is not beyond the pale. Black and white are prepared to work together to find new solutions as is evident in the Buthelezi Commission and KwaZulu/Natal Indaba proposals and the report of the S.A. Law Commission. The National Party, however, continues to have a stranglehold in politics which stifles the goodwill which exists in all population groups.

Groundswell pressures are building up in white society demanding that the Government face our problems realistically and if there was no hope of succeeding, I would not be doing what I am doing.

Church and politics – the need for an effective liberation theology   7

The Lord is my light and my salvation; whom shall I fear? the Lord is the strength of my life; of whom shall I be afraid?

Psalm 27

No work, however modest, on the future of South Africa would be complete, I think, without reference to the commitment of believers in the Christian faith in South Africa and of those of other religions, equally, who actively seek peace and unity and the abolition of the evils of racism.

This country has a remarkable history of many men and women over many generations who have courageously professed, each in their own way, the hallowed tenets of their creed during times and in circumstances which have been fraught with danger. I think here of Bishop John Colenso, Mahatma Gandhi, Albert Lutuli, Bishop Alphaeus Zulu, The Rev. S.D. Simelane, Canon Xaba, Archbishop Joost de Blank, Archbishop Denis Hurley, Bishop Thomas Savage, Dr Beyers Naude, Dr Alan Paton and others too numerous to mention. They have spoken out for justice and for His will to triumph when the forces of darkness have been very forbidding and when others more powerful have used the scriptures in their own way to justify that which is inherently wrong.

I am an Anglican and I constantly seek the word of God because I could not go on without Him. I have been privileged to have had among my spiritual advisors and confidants men of the calibre of the late Bishop Alphaeus Zulu and the former Archbishop of Cape Town, Bill Burnett. When everything around me seemed bleak and full of despair they have comforted me and counselled wisely.

Peace on earth and goodwill to all men, as conveyed by St. Luke in his description of the birth of our Lord, encapsulates, for me, the essence of the meaning of our life here on earth.

The message that God conveyed to us then – of reconciliation with each other and with Him around His son – are tidings which I believe should be uppermost in the minds of all South Africans now as we look to our future.

We need to heed the words of Paul, the Apostle to the Corinthians, when he said: 'To wit, that God was in Christ, reconciling the world unto himself, not imputing their trespasses unto them; and hath committed unto us the word of reconciliation.' (2 Corinthians, Chapter 5 v. 19.)

There is no better time than now for us to seek this reconciliation with each other and with our God. He created us all equal in His image and I believe we all can reach out to each other and dismantle the man-made divisions between us. He created us to love and He created us to be equal so that we can love equally.

Apartheid and racism has sown its divisive seed throughout South Africa and various churches and their believers too have often been divided, along with politicians and others, over tactics and strategies best able to bring us a new and better society or, for some, disastrously maintaining the status quo.

The Church in South Africa is still divided and this country's Church leadership does not speak with one voice. Church leaders these days all too frequently leap into political confrontation, taking one side against another. Some work within the Church to identify it with passing political bandwagons, and pass absolute judgments on those who dare to think differently to themselves. What grieves me is that those that do involve themselves in party political strife have often moved away from local church congregations in their journeys into politics.

I am confused by some Church leaders acting as political powers in South Africa because I have always known that there is no salvation through politics!

Nevertheless, the Church in South Africa is still a place where real war is being waged against racism. It is a place where gains in the fight against racism have sent out trend-setting influences into society at large. The Church is still struggling to find its true identity in this society of ours which is still in the process of becoming what it ought to be. The Church, too, is in a phase of transition.

The Church has a vital role to play in South Africa in calming fears and giving people the courage to meet difficulties head on. The Church can reconcile the far left and the far right. The message of the Gospel is a message which intimately relates to the question of good neighbourliness. The Church can give moral succour and it can help turn people away from killing and encourage them, instead, to talk.

As someone who occupies a leadership role, I know that all authority ultimately derives from God and if we abuse that gift, then we sin indeed.

In Christian terms we need to define South Africa's problems in such a way that the authority those of us do exercise is authority exercised in the name of God. We should also seek consensus about what Christian responsibility implies to each of us in our own sphere. We need to develop a national perception of the will of God for our country.

I am not a theologian and when I talk about the Church/State relationship, I talk about it from the point of view of a black leader who is a Christian caught up in a cross-fire between those who make radically different demands on the Church and those who expect different things from the State and conceive of the ideal Church/State relationship altogether differently.

Society is an immensely complex totality in which the authority structures in Government, churches, business, industry and elsewhere, interlock with each other, with immense ramifications, to produce a nation which is either healthy or sick.

I believe that nowhere before in the history of this country have so many been so ready to agree that South Africa needs to be healed of its racist wounds.

There is widespread consensus that loving one's neighbour as oneself, and doing unto others as you would have them do unto you, are practical impossibilities in a race-ridden apartheid society. We all want to escape from the straitjacket of racial sterility but, quite frankly, to date South Africans as people seem unable to put deed to work. We have the strange anomaly that there is a perceived need for change but an inability to do what we know has to be done.

Christians and others need to go beyond the reasoning and analyses of why we are not moving forward fast enough and apportioning blame wherever we find it. We need, instead, to each find the final authority for what we do in the authority we exercise in God. It is obedience to God which ultimately liberates us and makes us able to love.

St. Paul tells us that as Christians we can say anything to each other as long as we do so in love. The bitter rhetoric in black politics, between churchmen and others, including myself, does not often reflect this love.

In his letter to the Ephesians (Chapter 4, verses 29 to 32) St Paul writes: 'Do not let any unwholesome talk come out of your mouths, but only what is helpful in building others up according to their needs, that it may benefit those who listen . . . Get rid of all bitterness, rage, anger, brawling and slander, along with every form of malice. Be kind and compassionate to one another, forgiving each other, just as Christ God forgave you.'

There is a kind of desolation in many parts of South Africa which only a return to Christ can remedy. No politics in the world can restore the lack of dignity which comes from deviating from the will of God. It is God's forgiveness that we require.

When people lash out and kill because they are oppressed, to me that makes them the final victim of oppression and incapable of loving.

I am totally convinced that none of us is ever left by God so desolate that we are incapable of love. But we have got to have the desire to love before we can love. We are created as moral human beings with a capacity of that desire and we can spurn a desire, we can turn our back on it, but we can love if we desire to do so.

The vast majority of blacks have not turned to hating. They want the circumstances in which love dominates between race groups.

Churchmen, theologians, religious pressure groups and organisations and many others in this field both nationally and internationally visit me regularly. Some high-ranking men of God in this country and abroad try to avoid meeting me. They have made up their minds about me and about my brand of politics and they shun me, encouraging others to do likewise. I feel only their distance and disapproval. There is no Christian commitment to heal wounds and to seek each other as brothers in Christ and this troubles me greatly.

It is more often than not an uplifting and joyous experience to break bread and pray with brothers and sisters who come to share the word of God with me and to discuss differing perspectives of South Africa's problems and possible solutions. Other Christians come with judgmental attitudes, defined agendas, and an alarming unwillingness to hear other points of view. They are often nasty, partisan, mean and hurtful. The sense of fellowship which should be there whenever Christian meets Christian to look at life and death issues, is not there.

I share these thoughts in this book because when clerics, and particularly theologians, make serious errors of judgment, consequences can be dire. I am not saying that they should agree with me and that I am always right. I am saying that I perceive that for some compassion has been compartmentalised and that universal love, Christian succour and support is shared sparingly.

From time to time I get the uneasy feeling that some of the clerics and theologians I meet would be much more at home talking to revolutionaries about Christ in a bloody revolution than they would be in talking about Christ as the King of Peace working on all sides of all warring factions.

This is why, as a layman, I find myself forced to ask questions about the Western Christian conscience of some learned theologians. There is that in the Gospel which predisposes believers to side with the oppressed and with the poorest of the poor. I understand this and I praise God for it. However, when some Western guilt perceptions, resulting from the eras of slavery and colonial exploitation, lead to the glorification of the dramatic, then there is something wrong.

Because apartheid is as hideous as it is and oppression has endured for as long as it has, there is an unrecognised tendency among many Western thinkers to put some kind of mystique around freedom fighters who can be seen as fighting for noble ends. There is something more exciting about the sword used in holy battle than there is in the humility of the olive branch.

This guilt complex I mention is often carried over into religious and theological perceptions. Freedom fighters are seen as a breed apart.

There is a blindness to the actual intentions of placing a bomb on a street corner. There is a blindness to South African revolutionaries' real endeavours to bring about the ungovernability of South Africa by developing a people's war. There is a blindness to the real brutality of punitive economic sanctions against the South African Government which could well be thrusting the poorest of the poor beyond the reach of life itself in the future. There is an austerity of love in the theologians to whom I refer, who see God as involved in a vicious backlash of the oppressed and who is there with revolutionaries who are making ordinary men, women and more tragically children, the cannon fodder of their campaigns.

I have a vision of South Africa in which many things are delicately poised but I believe that black, white, Indian and Coloured can eventually peacefully establish decency and democracy.

We can, of course, fail. God has given us the right to fail. It is therefore not certain that the things I believe in will come to pass. There are finely balanced scales; there are delicately poised forces and counter-forces. There is no certainty; there is only faith.

This is why I am often appalled when theologians and senior churchmen thrust a spear into the delicacy of the human balance in which we find ourselves. At times I feel that they have put many of us in South Africa under analytical microscopes and only see us through the lenses that they have shaped. I do not find some of them sitting by my side, standing in my shoes, aching with my pain and looking at the world through my eyes. There is more often than not an austerity which denies empathy.

In my dealings with some theologians I find that they can theologise and theorise about things I have to do, whether I like them or not. I tell them that I often find myself in a position in which the buck has stopped at my desk, issues are there to confront me and I have to say yes or no and I have to make one decision or another. In the loneliness of that position I often have to inwardly cry out for God's guidance because the world is often altogether too mysterious for me to understand.

I come from peasant stock and even today I live in a peasant society and as the Chief of the Buthelezi clan, I also play a leadership role in peasant society. Leading at the level of the KwaZulu Government and Inkatha, I am confronted with some of the best brains in the world and some of the most erudite thinking in the world. I cannot help but be aware of the disparity between homespun peasant wisdom and the wisdom of the learned.

Generally speaking, I find no real problem in reconciling the Third World elements of my existence with the First World elements. One of the real problems I face is that of dealing with those who are too clever by half, too learned for the limitations of their own human understanding and too dogmatic in what they say.

I have learnt to recognise the danger of heeding the man or woman who speaks in terms of categoric imperatives. I have learnt that whenever people talk with the kind of erudition which spices everything that is said with absolutes, danger is at work around me.

This is why from my perspective of life I have to constantly cling to the conscious knowledge that it is Christ who directs the affairs of South Africa and that it is He who is leading this country to its divinely appointed ends. It is Christ's kingdom on earth that we should be striving for.

The realisation of Christ directing the final developments of mankind and just as certainly mankind in South Africa, makes me realise the extent to which He is there in the camps of my enemies, reconciling men and women to Himself and laying His love before those who despise Him in sin. It is this realisation of Christ being actively involved in His divine work on every side of every conflict in this country that gives such particular importance to the rejection of those who deal in absolutes.

For me Christ is the Reconciler and knowing my own confessed sin and my salvation from the consequences of sin through the grace of God, I cannot identify my enemy as a Godless enemy. Christ has not taken sides among those who are in bitter opposition to each other. He works among all demanding reconciliation, demanding everything that the Gospel should mean to us in our daily lives.

The image of Christ being everywhere in every race group, in every political group, attempting to reconcile people across every political division in our polarised society, cautions me to heed the wisdom of the most oppressed and the poorest of the poor. I make this jump back into my earlier contrast of my peasant background and my leadership environment because I must reconcile these two worlds. Christ reconciles them. He is there in both. So must I be.

I tell the theologians I referred to earlier that it may be that when none are left to care for reconciliation, and to work for it because everybody has been pushed beyond their human endurance, we can talk about the justification of revolution or theorise about holy wars. While Christ is there on every side of every conflict in this country, however, revolutionary violence can only violate the temples of God in which Christ is at work.

I made the point earlier that I am the kind of person who is the subject matter of theological speculation and theorising. I have to do so while they can think. I have to make decisions while they can debate the wisdom of the decisions that are made. I have to live out the limitations of my humanity and burden perhaps the whole of South Africa with the consequences of my errors or, pray God, some benefits of sometimes doing the right thing.

112

There is no easy solution that I know of to our problems and there is no final overnight outworking of the traumatic development of the relationships between the State and the Church in South Africa. We are busy discovering the meaning of the Gospel in our day and age and in our changed circumstances. It is as though we are having to make the Gospel come alive by the grace of God in our society.

This image immediately demands the humility to realise that the messengers of God are not all located in my own camp. When God cries out 'Who will go for me and whom will I send?' there are responses across the boundaries which divide political camps. Divine callings in one sphere of South African life are different to divine callings in another sphere.

Every day of my political life I have to contend with the consequences of deep anger tormenting individuals and endangering their humanity. I lead among a people who know the deprivation at which the civilised world shudders. Some are pushed too far.

It is these people who are transformed into the cannon fodder of those who plot the circumstances in which they can rise to power and fame as they send wave after wave of the poorest of the poor and the most oppressed to die in the pursuit of their political luxuries.

This is a harsh thought but such leadership does exist in circumstances which apartheid authors – the circumstances beyond human caring among those who have been pushed beyond their human endurance. Had I a mind to become a demagogue to prey on my fellow human beings, it is those who are pushed beyond their human endurance on whom I would prey. I wonder sometimes how one finally distinguishes between such demagoguery and the valiant employer of violence in a just war. I cannot make that distinction and I believe that too many make it too glibly.

We in our circumstances have perhaps an emphasised need for a liberation theology that actually works. The obvious contrast of the First World/Third World circumstances of people in South Africa screams out for equality for all. When everybody is starving, nobody is to blame but when half are starving and half are obese with over-consumption, then who is to blame? Is the liberation theology we search for a theology of a pointing finger and a directing of blame across this hideous line which divides the poorest of the poor from the over-affluent?

Or is a true liberation theology a theology which pursues the dangers of sin on both sides of the haves/have-nots dividing line? Is Christ not busy on both sides of this line?

All perception surely leads to the recognition of the innocence of the oppressed but all faith says that both the oppressed and the oppressor need salvation in Christ and both the oppressed and the oppressor must be joined into the task forces that can bring the Kingdom of God on earth as it is in Heaven.

There is in our society, I think, the danger that those who feel so much pain sometimes go far out ahead of others who suffer equally. The suffering masses then amount to no more than some kind of distant past base from which they were launched. The suffering of others is somehow left behind.

It is all too easy to justify anything way out front because of the hideousness of that which lies behind.

I do not understand the mystery of suffering and pain. I do not understand why Christ created a world in which the meek shall inherit the earth and the poor and the oppressed are blessed in a way that those who cannot pass through the eye of a needle are not blessed.

I can only follow my own Christian conscience and I can only grapple with the meaning of the Gospel and I can only attempt to rediscover the meaning of the Gospel in my own day and age in my own environment.

We all have to seek to understand God's mind in very perplexing circumstances. God is God. He created the world and He appoints the destinies of nations. He gives us the visions to do the right thing and the strength to do it.

Sanctions and disinvestment 8

There is only one firm statement that I can make on disinvestment, that I will have nothing to do with it. I will not, by any written or spoken word, give it any support whatsoever.

The late Dr Alan Paton, author of Cry the Beloved Country

*T*he question of whether or not economic sanctions against South Africa are constructive in registering the West's opposition to apartheid is controversial. In every Western country there are divisions between those who favour sanctions and those who oppose them.

I always ask what do the majority of black South Africans want? Their decision must be my decision. They don't want sanctions and disinvestment. They want jobs, not hunger, and they say so. I do not know of one black worker throughout South Africa who has voluntarily left his place of foreign-investor employment in support of sanctions. Black workers vote with their feet against disinvestment when they stand in queues outside the factory gates of foreign investors desperately seeking work.

According to the International Chamber of Commerce (ICC) more than 550 foreign companies have been obliged to divest their holdings in South Africa since 1985 because of pressure and sanctions policies. This had 'weakened the political and economic bargaining power of the country's black population,' it added in a submission to a United Nations' hearing in Geneva on the role of transnational business corporations in S.A. and Namibia. (The Star Bureau, London, September 6, 1989).

Not one foreign-owned factory still remaining in South Africa is out of production because blacks refuse to work in it. In fact, most blacks prefer employment in a foreign-owned factory because Western investors have led the field of black worker advancement and corporate responsibility. Black South African workers know that unless they have a job, their families will starve. That says it all.

I am therefore totally opposed to sanctions and disinvestment. Furthermore, there is no clarity on whether or not sanctions against South Africa will achieve the results that those who argue for them hope for. There is no agreement about what the actual consequences of economic sanctions will be. More importantly, there are strong dissenting voices in South Africa which disagree with sanctions as measures which will assist in the struggle for liberation.

For every pro-sanctions advocate including high media profile churchmen like Anglican Archbishop Desmond Tutu and the President of the World Alliance of Reformed Churches, the Rev. Allan Boesak, there are scores of others who oppose economic action who do not receive the same international publicity. They are no lesser foes of apartheid than Archbishop Tutu and the Rev. Boesak.

Within Archbishop Tutu's own church there are many concerned Anglicans who strongly oppose his stand on this issue. A Resources Study conducted for the Anglican Diocese of Johannesburg, for instance, noted in part the following: 'There is widespread fear that the impact of the Archbishop's high political profile in calling for sanctions and the isolating of South Africa from the rest of the world will seriously jeopardise the capacity of the diocese.

'The backlash is already affecting the diocese as members apply sanctions against the Church by withdrawing or limiting support . . . The Archbishop may be speaking as an individual and as a black man but this is clearly not the perception . . . the diocese is sharply divided over the issue of sanctions. Many seriously believe that sanctions will set back by 30 years the progress towards a more integrated society and could well increase rather than solve the problems of apartheid. Polarisation is likely to continue and become more serious unless there is more dialogue and appreciation that those who oppose sanctions do so for sincere reasons borne out of Christian conviction . . .' (Resources Study: Prepared by the Rev. Canon Peter Read, Everald Compton International).

116

Bishop Stanley Mogoba, President of the Methodist Church of Southern Africa and President of the South African Institute of Race Relations, speaks out forcefully against sanctions when he says that a solution for South Africa's problems must be based on sound research and analysis 'rather than emotions and pandering to political interest groups.'

Dr Mogoba told a meeting of the Interaction Council in Harare, Zimbabwe, that South Africans were 'the victims of political rhetoric, both from within the country and from foreign governments that ignore the truth . . .' Negotiation was the 'only viable option' and it was an option that did not 'lend itself with ease, as do violence and sanctions, to the political rhetoric of those who prefer to be swayed by their emotions than by the facts with which they are confronted . . .'

Church bodies representing millions of South Africans of all races have come out in strong opposition to sanctions and disinvestment. The Rev. M. L. Badenhorst, the President of the Full Gospel Church of God, with 500,000 members, about half of them blacks and with the largest Indian Christian community in the country, has been appointed chairman of a group of 970 church denominations and bodies opposed to sanctions.

Mr Sam Motsuenyane, chairman of the National African Federated Chamber of Commerce, says sanctions will result in mass black suffering. The American Chamber of Commerce in South Africa warns that sanctions and disinvestment has enriched the white local businesses while hurting blacks. The National President of the Jaycees in South Africa, Mr Vernon Matthysen, returned from the United States of America claiming pro-sanctions agitators were 'totally unwilling to listen to reason and did not care if sanctions resulted in unemployment and misery . . .' Black leaders and others opposed to them were labelled 'stooges of the system.'

Mrs Ina Perlman, the Executive Director of Operation Hunger, which is already feeding more than 1.5 million people in South Africa who would otherwise perish, has made numerous trips to the United States of America pleading against sanctions. Although Operation Hunger is not a political organisation and does not make political statements, Mrs Perlman says it believes it is imperative that the 'potentially disastrous consequences of negative economic action be made known . . .'

A special commission of the S.A. Catholic Bishops' Conference appointed to examine sanctions noted that economic pressures had 'clearly had a totally counter-productive effect on Government thinking' and that if sanctions were likely to produce a loss of vitally-needed jobs 'most blacks prove to be tentative about pressing the issue . . . it cannot be said that blacks overall favour sanctions and are prepared to endure the hardship, a view apparently held by a minority only . . .'

Authoritative unbiased research, including a substantial report by the influential Washington-based Investor Responsibility Research Centre, concludes that most black South Africans do not favour sanctions and disinvestment and support only comes from a 'hard core' minority measuring between 14 and 26 per cent.

A senior US official, Mr Charles Freeman, deputy to former Assistant Secretary of State, Dr Chester Crocker, disclosed at a Congressional hearing that black South African anti-apartheid activists were telling the US Government 'behind closed doors' that they had 'strong misgivings' about disinvestment.

As I noted earlier, anti-apartheid campaigner and veteran opposition politician, Mrs Helen Suzman, now retired, is vehemently opposed to sanctions as are numerous other anti-apartheid individuals and organisations throughout South Africa as well as the majority of the black masses. Why are we all, then, largely ignored in the West by people like Senator Edward Kennedy and others in the United States Congress and Senate? How can the hierarchy of the Anglican Church, at its Lambeth conferences, turn their backs on what blacks really want? Why do leaders of the Commonwealth and others in Europe, Australia, Canada and elsewhere do likewise? It is tragic that friends of the South African struggle for liberation so disregard the views and the sentiments of the majority of blacks who are the victims of apartheid.

Black South Africans fundamentally disagree with some Western observers who believe that the struggle against apartheid cannot peacefully succeed in bringing about radical change and establishing a just society. Black South Africans disagree that the recalcitrance of the South African Government spells the need for a holocaust and doom. We are the victims of apartheid; we are the oppressed.

The risks involved in applying economic sanctions against South Africa do not accord with our perceptions. We know that jobs lost will more often than not be jobs lost forever when companies pull out. We know that you cannot tinker with economies without risking serious consequences. For the outside world to perpetuate the myth that it can end apartheid through sanctions is merely prolonging the agony of the people in this country by offering false hopes and empty promises.

Why are some people so arrogantly insistent on telling blacks what is good for them and how much they are prepared to suffer? More and more, with increased spending power, blacks will be able to exert greater influence and have greater power as consumers in the South African economy. Maximising economic growth will maximise opposition to apartheid. Sanctions will make sure this never happens.

Black economic power, if it is allowed to happen, will become such a major factor that a rearrangement of the priorities of commerce and industry and infrastructural development and a realignment of social forces will have to take place to accommodate the contributory value of the upwardly mobile masses. Sanctions will make sure this never happens.

Sanctions are a recipe for violence and despair and they are the enemy of all who want this country to emerge as a united, non-racial, multi-party, free-enterprise democracy. We must do everything possible at every level to lay foundations for future economic development. It is madness to destroy these foundations. Sanctions do not build, they destroy. For blacks, the only dignity that there is in poverty is to be found among those who are doing something about their own poverty – lifting themselves up by their bootstraps.

There is a desperate need to salvage human dignity in the poverty that apartheid has thrust on black South Africa. Sanctions will not do this. Apartheid will ultimately fail because the human rights struggle is allied to economic reality which reinforces the struggle for liberation. Apartheid is economically unworkable and this makes it politically unworkable.

The single most important strategic objection to sanctions, noted by all opponents of economic action, is that they will slow down the pace at which the balance of economic power will shift in favour of blacks. If South Africa was no longer able to export coal, thousands of blacks would be out of work. Already, in the vehicle assembly, fruit, canning and sugar industries, to name a few, thousands of black workers are already unemployed.

It is estimated that about 60,000 jobs have already been lost as a result of disinvestment and another 150,000 as a result of lost international trade. Other figures are higher than these, which are conservative. These lost jobs are those of black workers and statistics show that each black breadwinner feeds from nine to 12 dependents. This means that more than two million black people are already worse off than before because of sanctions.

A new study has revealed that sanctions have already cost half a million jobs and a million more black people would be jobless if sanctions continue throughout the 1990s.

Mr Chris van Wyk, Chief Executive of Bankorp, revealed the results of a Trust Bank econometric calculation of the multiplier effects of sanctions. He said another decade of sanctions would render two million more black people destitute.

Mr van Wyk said about 500,000 fewer people were employed than could have been because of the many new jobs not created, as sanctions had stifled the South African economy.

At a symposium of the International Community, he said sanctions had also:

☐ Cost South Africa a cumulative R40 billion in foreign exchange, resulting in production losses of about R80 billion and total 'standard of living' losses of R100 billion;

☐ Cut real consumer spending 15 per cent and GDP about 10 per cent;

☐ Curtailed spending on education and health;

☐ Impaired South Africa's ability to reach its full export potential; and

☐ Radicalised blacks to the left and whites to the right, hampering political settlement.

He said the total multiplier effect of sanctions and disinvestment was equivalent to a halving of the gold price between 1985 and 1989. (*Business Day*, November 3, 1989.)

International experience has been that poverty radicalises, criminalises, is a health hazard and undermines youth education. These effects are already very apparent in South Africa's black townships. Men, women and children are starving in South Africa. It is incomprehensible to me that Christian, political and trade union leaders can press for more economic sanctions when those already imposed are causing such suffering.

120

Sanctions inflict a cost on whites too but their generally higher level of saving gives them a safety net which simply does not exist for blacks.

Mr John Kane-Berman of the South African Institute of Race Relations notes that as long as the illusion persists that the outside world can end apartheid through sanctions, it strengthens one of the greatest obstructions to action for change. 'This is the belief that black people are powerless and that they must therefore rely on others to bring about changes on their behalf,' he said.

Mr Kane-Berman told a US Congressional sub-committee examining sanctions proposals – which subsequently ignored his advice – that there was 'no doubt' that sanctions, if effectively imposed, would mean more black people out of work and an increase in the incidence of malnutrition and black infant mortality, already eleven times that among whites.

Noting that there was a school of thought that starving blacks would rise up in revolt, he suggested that this was doubtful. Nevertheless, even if they did, 'they would face a security apparatus already immeasurably strengthened by sanctions because they forced it to become self-sufficient in every item of armament it needs to suppress internal revolt, not to mention its capacity to inflict enormous costs elsewhere on the sub-continent.'

He cogently added that while they posed no real threat to the security of the State, these blacks would certainly pose a threat to a black trade union movement already worried that the growing reserve army of unemployed could undermine the bargaining power that it had won against heavy odds.

There is substantial evidence which shows that a growing economy generates forces which blacks can harness to empower themselves to do the job of dismantling apartheid and the results of this were shown in previous chapters: rising wages have enabled people to move out of overcrowded townships into white cities and suburbs; increasing levels of education and skills have forced a policy change with regard to black unions; the availability of more jobs and better incomes in urban as compared with rural areas; action and organisation.

Foreign influences can help blacks in this task – but only if they do nothing to undermine black empowerment. Sanctions will undermine the most important non-violent weapon that black people have at their disposal, their labour power. Black people constitute 65 per cent of the economically active population and an increasing proportion of the national work-force's skilled component.

Over the years I have addressed hundreds of thousands of black South Africans at mass rallies. Not once, when I have asked whether they support sanctions and disinvestment, have they replied in the affirmative. I know of no mass membership organisation which is democratically structured and which has an elected leadership directly answerable to the people which endorses sanctions.

It is black spokesmen in the South African Council of Churches, the United Democratic Front, the Congress of South African Trade Unions and other organisations working under their umbrella and who work in tandem with them, who call for sanctions. Not one of them is directly answerable to a mass membership organisation. They are all chosen for office by committees which are themselves not elected committees. These organisations work as the internal wing of the External Mission of the ANC.

The African National Congress, with its pro-violence factions, calls for sanctions. The vast majority of blacks who travel the world drumming up support for sanctions do so in part because they are committed to destroying the free-enterprise system in South Africa. This is understandable because as I have already noted, they see the destruction of the South African economy as a necessary step that must be taken before apartheid can be eradicated. It is very significant that black leaders who are most committed to using revolutionary violence to bring about a one-party socialist State call the loudest for sanctions.

The reality is that blacks in cities and towns and villages throughout South Africa are entirely dependent on their weekly pay packets to survive. For them it is absurd to support moves to diminish employment opportunities in circumstances in which there is already a very high level of unemployment and under-employment.

The Universal Declaration of Human Rights says that everyone has the right to life, that no one should be subject to inhuman treatment, that everyone has the right to work and the right to an adequate standard of living. I add my voice to all the others who believe that international action that puts people out of work is a violation of these clauses of the Declaration.

I remember well the words of my late friend, the internationally acclaimed author Dr Alan Paton, who wrote: 'I take very seriously the teachings of the Gospel, in particular the parables about giving drink to the thirsty and food to the hungry. It seems to me that Jesus attached supreme – indeed sacred – significance to such actions. Therefore, I will not help to cause any such suffering to any black person . . . I am told that this is a simplistic understanding of the teachings of the Gospel. Let it be so. That is the way I choose to understand them.

'I am also told that I am ignoring the views of those black South Africans who support disinvestment. Most of these black South Africans will not be the ones to suffer hunger and thirst. Many of them are sophisticated, highly educated, safely placed. I also know sophisticated and highly educated black men and women who will have nothing to do with disinvestment. I choose to associate myself with them.

'I am told that, although I believe my views to be moral, they are, in fact, immoral because I will not take the side of those black people who want disinvestment. This is a new interpretation of morality to me, that I ought to adopt certain views because some influential black people hold them. I do not hold these views because they are acceptable – or not acceptable – to either black people or white people. I do not consider that the welfare of black people or the welfare of white people is the supreme consideration. The supreme consideration to me is the welfare of my country and therefore the welfare of all its people . . .

'There is an often-heard declaration: "We do not mind suffering. We are used to suffering." But this again is often the declaration of those who will suffer least. To put it briefly, my conscience would not allow me to support disinvestment. For I must ask myself – and my readers who are concerned to do what is right – how long must the suffering it would cause go on before the desired end is achieved? A month? Two months? A year? Five or 10 years perhaps?' (Dr Alan Paton, *Save the Beloved Country*, a collection of speeches and articles. Hans Strydom Publishers).

Even if it has to be recognised that there is a division of opinion among blacks about the merits of sanctions and disinvestment, other considerations when thought out properly argue against them as an anti-apartheid strategy. For the sake of convenience I present these considerations under a number of headings:

The application of measures to prohibit investment in South Africa cannot work.

It is not possible to mount a blockade against South Africa and it is also not possible to ensure that one Western enterprise does not step into the vacuum of an enterprise which withdraws its investment. The vast network of international holdings and reciprocal business relationships always makes it possible for companies to restructure their business relationships with South Africa. For example, Coca Cola has withdrawn, but millions of bottles of Coca Cola are still sold in South Africa. IBM has withdrawn, but there are many thousands of IBM personal computers and other IBM products on sale and in operation. Barclays Bank has withdrawn, but under the name of First National Bank continues to be a leading South African bank.

Business adjustments that are made can protect the businessman but it does not imply that retrenchments do not take place and that black workers do not suffer despite the successful manoeuvres of business to protect its interests.

We have the classical case of the immunity of white South Africa to economic sanctions in the arms embargo. Not even a decade after a mandatory arms embargo was introduced against South Africa, the country became a major net exporter of arms and is earning a significant proportion of money derived from all exports through the sales of arms and equipment.

Neighbouring States which support sanctions and disinvestment in South Africa continue to be major trading partners of South Africa. For every market lost another is sought. For every trade link closed, another is opened. Disinvestment is just not enforceable.

Maximising economic growth will maximise opposition to apartheid.
Disinvestment is a measure which must be judged in a correct time-scale perspective. Like revolution, if it could be short, sharp and successful, we would be facing one set of considerations but it may not be and then we face an entirely different set of considerations. There will be no overnight victory in South Africa. There will be no leap into Utopia from whence we could rapidly undo the harm that revolution and sanctions will cause.

Apartheid will fail, as I have said. In every oppressed society it is the rising middle class reaching ceilings in vertical mobility that generates political leadership and power.

Black bargaining power increases in times of economic growth. Black/white worker substitution and black/white manager substitution increases in times of economic growth. White dependence on blacks increases in times of economic growth.

Capacities to adjust to economic sanctions.
The South African Government has a vast battery of possible adjustments it can make to immunise the white electorate from the harsh effects an effective sanctions campaign can have. Large corporations can make adjustments. In these adjustments the price of failed sanctions is shifted ever-increasingly lower and lower down the social scales until blacks pay the cost.

The scale of successful sanctions.
For sanctions to work as effective coercive measures against Pretoria they would have to be both mandatory and very comprehensive. They would have to be so comprehensive and so rigorously applied that they would end up destroying the foundations of future economic growth. Economies cannot be switched on and off at will and the final effect of really successful sanctions against South Africa would leave any post-apartheid government without the means to govern.

The political vulnerability of the ruling National Party.
Economic development in South Africa has done more than create the circumstances in which apartheid cannot work. It has led to the need to induct blacks into skilled jobs hitherto preserved for whites. It has led to the granting of freedom of movement to blacks so that limited skilled human resources are available where they are needed and it has led to the granting of trade union rights to blacks to ensure sound industrial relations.

Economic development in South Africa has not only benefited an ever-increasing number of blacks but it has also challenged some of the fundamentals of apartheid and it has created a political crisis for the ruling National Party.

Apartheid as a formalisation of racism which was the aftermath of the colonial period came into existence to serve vested Afrikaner interests after the National Party won its first election in 1948. Apartheid was developed and shaped to put whites as the sole decision-makers in the country. Conformity to the demands of apartheid was both easy and rewarding in its initial decade of development. Whites, particularly Afrikaners, gathered together in solidarity under apartheid and reaped the rewards as special beneficiaries of State policy.

As economic development continued apace, however, the South African economy became ever more dependent on forces outside the control of the South African Government. Foreign markets, the need for imported technology and management skills and the need for imported capital all combined to make an ever-increasing number of Afrikaners less dependent on the Government in the preservation of their vested interests.

After further economic development the situation developed into one in which the Government actually became a liability in the preservation of the vested interests of a significant proportion of Afrikaners. They could no longer look to their Church and the State to serve their interests and industrial development which became dependent upon resources, influence, money, technology, markets and governments which were all hostile to apartheid, created a whole new class of Afrikaners who challenged Afrikanerdom from within.

These economic factors were, in the dynamics of the totality of society, related to social and political factors which produced new ferment in white politics. The Government recalcitrance which the West so fears is now being challenged by a growing number of Afrikaners within the ruling National Party.

The power of the ruling National Party is crumbling and I want to emphasise this point. Ribald racism rejects the moves the South African Government has had to make to meet the demands of economic imperatives and supports the move to the right. The move to the right is itself becoming a threat to the vested interests of those who want to remain at the centre and those who are moving to the left of the National Party. For the first time in the history of the National Party there is serious internal dissent and rising tensions.

The greater the economic development of South Africa, the more vulnerable the National Party's leadership becomes to the final outcome of the conflict between its left and its right. The more National Party members perceive South Africa to be threatened from without, the slower this process of internal readjustment will become. The threat of sanctions and the threat of violent onslaughts impairs the process which will inevitably end up creating the pressures which will ensure that the Government becomes less recalcitrant and more amenable to political reason.

White South Africa is not, as revolutionaries want the world to believe, beyond redemption and however true it is that apartheid cannot be reformed, it is a reality that white society can be reformed and that white political thinking can be made more responsible.

126

It is also true that blacks and whites, as I have stressed, are recognising that they have common cause in wanting a normalised South Africa. A rising tide of opinion in black and white society is demanding the normalisation of South Africa as a modern Western-type industrial democracy. More and more whites are concurring with blacks that the preservation of the free-enterprise system is vital and that the only way this can be ensured is by dismantling apartheid.

Whites are beginning to see the writing on the wall that apartheid cannot preserve white vested interests and that the social, political and economic separation of South Africa's race groups constitutes a threat to their vested interests.

All these considerations demand that Western observers recognise that the recalcitrance of the South African Government can best be changed by stimulating factors inside South Africa which are best placed to ensure that the Government's vulnerability is countered by moving forward in the direction the West itself wants for South Africa.

The responsibilities of Western industrial democracies.
There may well be conflict between international capitalism and international socialism and it might well be that Western countries in the final analysis have a responsibility to ensure that the underdeveloped Third World escapes the social and economic consequences of poverty. When, however, I think of South Africa's future and when I think of the future of the whole of Southern Africa, I argue the merits of the free-enterprise system simply because it is the most effective system mankind has yet developed to bring about the kind of economic development that is so desperately needed on this sub-continent.

As I have observed, those who campaign the loudest for disinvestment are the most committed to bringing about change through revolutionary violence or to bringing about change by making South Africa ungovernable in order to establish a socialist State in this country. Poverty really is a fatal enemy of democracy. There are already levels of poverty in South Africa which will make it very difficult for any government whatever its ideological persuasion to govern in such a way that the majority of the people are satisfied that political change has brought about sufficient improvements in their living circumstances.

If a democratic government is established in South Africa which does not have the means to govern for the benefit of the people and does not satisfy their aspirations, it will soon be under siege. I have said this before but it is germane to my whole thinking about the future of South Africa and is the key to my vision of a new South Africa.

If not sanctions, what else?
So, if not sanctions, what else? There is only one answer: alternate economic action aimed at bringing about a liberated and democratic South Africa. A feasible plan of action could be drawn up to achieve the following objectives:

☐ The economic upliftment of blacks and increased spending power which would arrest their present poverty and curb poverty-related behaviour such as rapidly diminishing cultural values and communal violence.

☐ Greatly increased educational opportunities for blacks.

☐ An environment which is more conducive to family life and community development.

☐ The social integration of all South Africa's race groups.

☐ A redistribution of wealth.

☐ The elimination of racial discrimination.

☐ The stimulation of job creation.

☐ Elimination of the exploitation of labour.

☐ Peaceful protests against apartheid.

☐ Enhancement of the quality of life for blacks.

☐ The encouragement of industrial decentralisation to stimulate economic growth in rural communities.

I ask the West to consider a conditional trade and investment strategy as an alternative plan of action to sanctions which could address all these stated objectives. It could offer substantial benefits to all major participants including overseas investors, foreign governments, the S.A. business community and all the people of sub-Saharan Africa – not only black South Africans.

The chairman of the Anglo American Corporation, Mr Gavin Relly, in an annual report, noted that the attainment of a five per cent growth rate was regarded as fundamental to South Africa's future. He said: 'Justice and equity do not flourish in conditions of poverty, whatever the politics of the party in power. South Africa will never be able to muster the resources needed to provide decent living standards and opportunities for its growing population unless it can attract foreign investment, as distinct from institutional aid.

'Foreign capital will still not flow here, even after apartheid has been abolished, if that otherwise desirable state of affairs should be brought about by means so violent as to leave behind an economic wasteland ruled – as history shows it would be – by extremists opposed to private capital and property.'

Postscript
Negotiations now –
who will make or break them?

At long last, much of what I have called for over the years as necessary preconditions before the process of true negotiations can start, have come to pass: Dr Nelson Mandela is now a free man, other political prisoners have been released, and various political parties and organisations unbanned and permitted to operate openly.

I was over-joyed at Dr Mandela's unconditional release and it is my fondest hope that we can walk together into a new and democratic South Africa. As he returned to his family and to work for his country, I asked that our tribute to him be the one he would most want: the tribute of black unity. I called on black South Africa to form the national unity on which a black national will could be mounted to use politics for the benefit of ordinary people throughout the country regardless of race. Sadly, to date, this has not been evident.

These are early days in the euphoria over the death-knell of apartheid and hopes of tangible reform. Expectations are high and concurrently there are tensions. Individuals and organisations are jockeying for position, as they have every right to do, to be in line along with the Government and others in authoring our future.

Now is surely the time for multi-party constructive input and not hardline 'them and us' dialogue between so-called ultimate contenders in a win-or-lose political battle. We must all be winners – South Africa must come first.

I see real dangers in the kind of politics that attempt to intimidate and force South Africans into specific party-political and ideological camps. People must be free to choose, they must be free to differ. Now, instead of this, those who do wish to stand their own ground face deliberate attempts to annihilate them politically.

Certain journalists, for instance, write openly that some black leaders who ignore overtures to align themselves with the ANC 'risk being swept aside ignominiously and dumped into the historical rubbish bin.' (Patrick Laurence, *The Star*, March 3, 1990) This is not the thinking on which democracies are founded.

Mr Terror Lekota, of the United Democratic Front, told reporters outright in Washington recently that the ANC/UDF was out to 'kill' me politically and that the collective leadership of the 'Mass Democratic Movement' was not in favour of any meetings between myself and Dr Mandela.

So there we have it. The gauntlet, to some extent, has been thrown down. Black unity, for certain people, is not a priority and it is clear that they intend to attempt to crush individuals and organisations that do not toe their line. All the signs are already with us.

I state now that this is not a situation of my own choosing or Inkatha's. How others wish to face the onslaught is up to them; I cannot speak or act for them. Some I know to be frightened men and women and the way things are going they have every reason to be. Their voices will be silenced; they will not be heard from again.

Inkatha holds out a hand of friendship to all while having the strength and the determination to continue to advocate its beliefs openly. We seek to work in the broader and democratic political context of having an equal right to put our aims and objectives to all the people of this country along with everybody else. Attempts to 'smash' us and 'deprive Inkatha of its political base' (as stated objectives in official ANC documents) have only hardened our resolve to seek a real multi-party system of government for our country.

We ask all organisations and leaders to see the need for across-the-board valuable input into the negotiations that lie ahead. We simply cannot comprehend that this will not be in the best interests of South Africa. This is not diverting the struggle for liberation, as we have been accused. We see it as a way of ensuring meaningful consensus and lasting national peace and stability. But, then again, Inkatha is not playing winner-takes-all politics.

As I write this I have just returned from abroad and from meetings with Prime Minister Margaret Thatcher and President George Bush. A Press conference was held on my arrival.

The questioning from some reporters was not how I and Inkatha saw our contribution to the emerging process of negotiations in this country but, instead, aggressive queries (almost accusations implying traitorous behaviour) as to why Inkatha had not 'joined' the African National Congress. There is a perception being peddled by some that only the ANC can negotiate a new South Africa into existence.

I pose the question: Is the ANC prepared to join a political process in which they will be one of a number of political parties negotiating with the Government? I further question whether it would be in the best interests of South Africa for there to be a bi-polar ANC/S.A. Government negotiating situation. Too few are really analysing why the ANC is insisting on their Harare Declaration which gives them ground to adopt confrontational positions and why they are still clamouring for the retention of punitive measures against South Africa.

Somewhere along the line the point is being missed by many here and abroad that national unity in South Africa does not have to be based on obedience to a specific party. What has happened so recently in the Eastern bloc and in the Soviet Union are lessons that have not, to date, been learnt by some here. It will be to our cost if they are not.

The Harare document is the first example of what could become a dangerous trend during the politics of negotiation in South Africa. The ANC met in Harare and drew up the Harare Declaration. It took this Declaration to the Organisation of African Unity and had it endorsed there. It was then taken to the Non-Aligned Countries and again it was endorsed. Finally, it was taken to the United Nations where its substance was endorsed with minor reservations.

The ANC is now tabling this Declaration as a document which purports to have real international acclaim and support. This is not a people's document. It has not been endorsed by the people of South Africa. It makes assumptions about the supremacy of the ANC and was drawn up to reflect the assumption that the only negotiations of any importance in South Africa will be negotiations between the ANC and the S.A. Government.

The ANC is a party among parties in South Africa. Attempts to create a perception of negotiations between the Government and the ANC, with all other Parties lining up behind one or the other, must be thwarted now. If this is insisted on, it will bedevil the whole political process of change in South Africa.

If it does continue to be the case, I warn now of troubled times ahead. I warn in the sense of the old Zulu folk tale of a herdboy who tells a passing stranger that there is a deadly snake around the next bend and to be careful that it does not rise up and strike him. The fact that the herdboy knew of the danger did not mean that he put the snake there.

There is an urgent need for Western governments to do everything that diplomacy can do to support developments in South Africa in which party political interests are bent to serve the interests of the State and of all South Africans. I am convinced that only a multi-party democracy, supported by both black and white, will survive in South Africa.

A lack of compromise and unwillingness to share and give-and-take on the part of some is already taking on ominous proportions. Violence throughout the country has exploded anew in some areas and continues unabated in others. It appals me. I completely denounce violence. I will go to my grave believing that non-violence and peaceful aims and objectives are primary, decent and worthwhile objectives which should be inculcated into the hearts and minds of all at all times.

Dimensions of a winner-takes-all conflict by those who are determined to eliminate opposition now in their quest for ultimate power are emerging daily. It is a tragic and extremely worrying situation. Calls, pleas and outright begging for calm, discipline and unity have not prevailed to any degree whatsoever. The killing, the arson, the looting continues.

As I greatly feared the myth of the 'armed struggle' of the ANC and the so-called 'right' of some to dispatch the 'enemy' as they see fit, has now reached over our borders and into our townships and cities.

The 'enemy' for many has become fellow blacks, who are being battered to death and intimidated for political, criminal and socio-economic reasons. Shops, homes, factories – all manner of facilities – are being burned to the ground in an orgy of spreading destruction. Battle zones and territories have been drawn. Families are fleeing their homes seeking refuge, safety and protection elsewhere. Many call for the police and the Army to move in. Others say they must stay out.

Thousands more breadwinners are now out of work because their places of employment are in ashes. This means that tens of thousands more who rely on the wages of these workers have no money to buy food, pay for rent and so on. Millions are now without any means of support in South Africa due to vast unemployment caused by economic and other conditions and considerably exacerbated by sanctions and disinvestment.

Some businessmen prepare to 'pack for Perth' while others frantically place billions of Rands off-shore far beyond the reach of those who talk of nationalisation and their understanding of the causes of the violence.

Behaviour once encouraged by the ANC as integral to the struggle for liberation (it was all right and often a duty to murder 'collaborators' and opponents, including town councillors, policemen, people like myself and anybody else targetted for assassination for whatever reason) is now reaping anarchy.

Violent youth, unemployed adults and others caught up in the chaos are out of control and even if the ANC does, at some stage, admit to regretting its militaristic stance, too much damage will already have been done. Smoke is in the air.

The simple facts are that no organisation can speak with two tongues. On the one hand the ANC says its armed struggle will continue (however ineffectually) and on the other it calls for guns and knives to be thrown into the sea in pursuit of black peace and unity. It talks of democracy while some of its spokesmen clearly attempt to force adherence to its views – quite certainly insofar as Inkatha is concerned. It can't work like that and now is the time for straight talk.

I had hoped to play down, in my earlier writing, the divisions between black leaders and organisations in the hope that once negotiations were made possible we would all concur and agree to abide by the tenets of fair play in politics as practised to a considerable degree in democracies throughout the world. I am not saying that the usual cut and thrust of competition will not play a part as they do everywhere. I am talking here of basic rights to put political options to the people for their ultimate acceptance or rejection. I had hoped, and still do, that multi-party strategies would quite naturally be acceptable to all. I hoped for too much as far as some people are concerned.

Now we will all have to wait and see. Democracy is waiting in the wings and the following is clear: wars are not won and one-party States are not established by playing marbles.

Business confidence is not encouraged by calls for nationalisation and the spectacle of burning buildings, butchered bodies, coups and out-of-control mob scenes. A vision of black and white getting on now with creating a new South Africa is rocked to the core and confusion and mistrust abounds when calls continue to be made, as Dr Nelson Mandela did in Stockholm, for world governments to drastically intensify sanctions and impose total diplomatic, cultural and sporting isolation on South Africa.

How will this pressure, as he claimed, Pretoria into accepting a peaceful negotiated settlement? Pretoria has already made it quite clear that it wants a peaceful, negotiated settlement. This is a task for us all to achieve.

I express now grave concerns about the consequences we will all suffer if far too many regard the struggle for liberation as a way of life and are not preparing themselves for the kind of politics that we will see around us in 1990. I warn about black leadership that is remote from the people who are crying out for peace and growing prosperity. Ultimately it is only real progress around the negotiating table which will defuse violence in South Africa and create equal opportunities for all.

The prime actors for negotiations have already been created by history and politics. The central stage on which they can act is already there. The audience is already seated and waiting.

What I am saying could perhaps provocatively be engineered to precipitate a confrontation between Dr Mandela and myself. This I do not want. In interviews Dr Mandela refers to me as his friend of many years and that is absolutely true. He has certainly had my friendship ever since I was a young man and he still has it. We will remain friends even if we do hold different positions at this juncture of South African political development. Even then it is only on a few issues on which I believe that we must agree to disagree.

When Dr Mandela talks about the need for the armed struggle to continue; when he talks about the need for nationalisation; when he likens Israel to South Africa; when he calls for intensified sanctions against South Africa and continued international pressure, he is not attacking me *per se*.

When I question these things, I am not attacking him *per se*. My respect for Dr Mandela is very profound. All I say is: 'My friend, you are very wrong on these issues. You are wrong for yourself, you are wrong for the ANC and you are wrong for South Africa. That is all. It does not diminish my love and respect for you and for the sacrifices that you have made for all of us.'

While Dr Mandela and I differ on some issues, and differ fundamentally on others, there is a great need for dialogue because there are some things that both he and I must be joined together in preserving. He has, for example, spoken sincerely of the need for black unity.

There is a broad South Africanism which will now emerge as friendly to democracy and Dr Mandela and I need to make quite sure that what either of us does separately, or what perchance we can do together, nurtures this new South Africanism.

Dr Mandela is now a free man and his own person and he can pursue his own tactics and strategies and set his own priorities. I am just as free and I can do just the same. If, however, the areas where we differ preclude dialogue and discussion of fundamental differences between us, then our several and joint under-achievement must only be laid at our own feet.

Differences between black and black are primarily differences about how to achieve and how to secure the values we hold in common and they are differences about what circumstances would best suit the preservation of the things we value in common. There are politically sound reasons why there must be black unity based on the acceptance of a multi-strategy approach. There are some things which if we do not either tackle together or help preserve together will run out of hand to be a danger to both of us.

Black South Africa has yet to get its act together and every action taken now by all concerned will have vast implications.

This is a time, I believe, for looking forward towards a Government of national unity and reconciliation. When I started writing this book nearly a year ago I had no idea of how quickly things would move. Nobody did. Some were caught completely off-guard and are now scrambling around trying to formalise and establish negotiating structures and positions. They harbour illusions of capturing the political high ground when in reality it should belong eventually to all South Africans.

I am in the fortunate position of standing right where I have always been and not having to move: in the middle ground along with the silent majority seeking decency and democracy and a peaceful end to racism. Inkatha has not had to make any adjustments to remain relevant to centre-stage politics. Its policy remains entirely intact and will not have to be changed for participation in this period of negotiation for which we have been working.

The ruling National Party and the S.A. Government have shifted precisely and directly towards our thinking in embracing and acting on the majority of the obstacles to negotiation Inkatha has outlined and articulated *ad nauseam* over the years. They talk now, as we have always done, of negotiations to end apartheid and of a multi-party, free-enterprise, democratic South Africa in which there will be equality of opportunity for all. Apologies are being made for the evils of apartheid; admissions of squandered, corrupt and ruthless power.

On the other side, the ANC and its affiliates can no longer talk in grandiose terms of seizing power and returning as a government from exile. They too appear to be moving, however, reluctantly and gradually, towards the political centre-field where the real dynamics of purposeful change will emanate.

If they do not participate in negotiations they will be out-manoeuvred and they know it. They can only attempt to smash them for their own ends. The irony is that the 'enemy' is forcing them (however subtly) to – as the saying goes – 'put up or shut up.' A whole new ball game has been put into play.

I say take the ball and run with it. There's no chance of being trapped by apartheid now. The State President cannot now go back on his word because if he did so it would unleash a tidal wave of anger and violence.

Let's get on with making people happy, making them secure in all ways. The ANC, instead, calls for continuing the armed struggle from abroad while in fact they can't even control uprisings and ongoing black violence (even though they claim superior support from the masses) within the country. Their plan to make South Africa ungovernable has sown bitter and unpalatable seeds. Whites are now looking with very wary eyes at the barbarous behaviour of some blacks and clearly wish they hadn't heard the political and economic pronouncements of others.

As I write this the ANC is seeking huge international financial backing to launch them on the road to building power bases and structures within South Africa. Whether similar resources will be forthcoming for fair contest and for other diverse political structures, including Inkatha, is another matter altogether. The West must be wary of loading the dice against multi-party choices being freely available to all South Africans.

If the world continues to support the politics of confrontation despite the fact that the South African Government has taken a giant step into the politics of reconciliation, I really do fear a white backlash.

However much the ANC and their publicists will shout and scream at the following assertion, they *are* being forced at present to move inch by inch, step by step, to where I stand – ready to participate in negotiations. This they cannot do while holding rifles in their hands and limpet mines in their briefcases. Sooner rather than later they will have to put their cards on the table. They will either be prepared to participate as equals or they will embark on a smash-and-grab campaign. Already supporters such as Archbishop Desmond Tutu and President Kenneth Kaunda have urged them to cease using violence as a political weapon, unfortunately to no avail. We have early indications. We have early warnings.

The ANC's idea of negotiations and mine differ drastically but, unlike me, they will sooner or later have to abandon the military accoutrement of their past power bases if they do indeed seek free and fair negotiations. I have always advocated jaw-jaw not war-war. They will have to do likewise or turn to unleasing hell on earth on this country. The West must analyse events and political posturing very carefully.

The ANC's Harare document clearly spells out the ANC's intention not to negotiate equally alongside the South African Government and others about the future of South Africa. They want the future to be decided in some kind of Constituent Assembly arrangement with the ANC as the dominant black factor. What the Harare document amounts to is a demand for the laying down of power by the South African Government and the ruling National Party taking its place as a party among parties. Political history has lessons in this regard which some have not read.

What they call for must be the end product of South African politics. It is an end, however, that must be negotiated to conclusion. South Africa is not Zimbabwe and I repeat, as I said elsewhere, that a Lancaster House-type conference will not be accepted by white South Africa. Likewise, South Africa is not Mozambique or Angola. Whites in South Africa, as noted earlier, have vast economic power, have superior military might. They control, whether we like it or not, the treasury and all manner of governmental and other structures. They are talking of a desire to share that power, because they know they will eventually have to.

They are thinking in terms of a process which will lead us to power-sharing.

We cannot risk a white backlash, caused by black ineptitude, halting the politics of negotiation. We cannot risk a black backlash caused by white ineptitude. Black South Africa, in the end, will get all that it wants and more if it plays its cards right.

There is something which runs very deep in my political soul and it is a real appreciation that political power based on anything other than acting out real mandates honestly received in real democratic consultations with the people, can only be passing power.

To this end Inkatha has drafted a document entitled *The 1990 Inkatha Declaration* which we believe, unlike the ANC's Harare Declaration, embodies the thinking and the spirit needed from black South Africa for us all to enter and finally conclude negotiations in such a way that the end result will be a truly democratic and unified South Africa.

The 1990 Inkatha Declaration

Preamble

Quite clearly South Africa is in the process of transition from an old apartheid society moving towards a true, multi-party democracy and in this historic ripeness of time, it is imperative that all patriots put the good of South Africa first and now demand of all political parties that they do so too.

The transition from an old order to a new order must be a people's transition and the negotiating process must incorporate all political parties.

There will be one South Africa with one people moving to but a single destiny and negotiation should strive to develop a constitutional model and aim at establishing not only political orders but also social and economic orders acceptable to the majority of people in the country.

A democratic political system to meet the requirements of South Africans

Whatever democratic system is finally adopted, in the politics of negotiation it is imperative that:

1. All the people shall be free in this their land of birth or land of adoption.

2. All the people shall have freedom of worship and all the churches and temples of the land shall be regarded as sacrosanct.

3. All the people shall participate in the governing of the country on the basis of total equality before the constitution and on the basis of universal adult suffrage through freely chosen representatives.

4. The rights of individuals shall be protected under the law regardless of race, colour, creed or sex.

5. There shall be an independent judiciary and the rule of law shall be protected by constitutional guarantees.

6. There shall be freedom of speech within the bounds of reason supported by practice and law in the civilised world and there shall be the right for all of freedom of opinion and expression and the right to propagate ideas through any media.

7. There shall be freedom of movement and residence within the borders of South Africa.

8. There shall be the right to freedom of peaceful assembly and association and there shall be no enforced membership of any association.

9. There shall be the right for all to work and the right of all to fair and just conditions of employment.

10. There shall be the right to form and join trade unions.

11. There shall be the right to equality of treatment by the State in all it does in the fields of law enforcement, social welfare and in education.

12. There shall be the right of parents to choose the kind of education they wish for their children and to seek private tuition when the education of the State does not meet with their approval.

13. There shall be the right to exercise rights and freedoms in such a way that everyone is subject only to such limitations as are determined by law solely for the purpose of securing due recognition and respect for the rights and freedoms of others and of meeting the just requirements of morality, public order and the general welfare in a democratic society.

14. There shall be the right for all to own fixed and movable property.

15. There shall be the right of protection from arbitrary arrest and the right of being arrested only for public hearing and all shall be regarded as innocent until proved guilty.

A democratic social system to meet the requirements of South Africans

16. There shall be the right of all to be treated with the respect properly befitting the status belonging to a unique creature of God and be treated with human dignity which shall be respected at all times.

17. There shall be the right of equal constitutional and legal status for all and all shall have the right of appeal to the courts of the land to uphold social equality.

18. There shall be the right of any member of any cultural group to preserve his or her culture and to put his or her culture into practice in ways limited only by desire to do so and by the legal restraints commensurate with the rule of law and the need to take reasonable steps to uphold the social order.

A free and equitable economic system

19. There shall be the right for all people to be free to pursue their entrepreneurial skills within the bounds of the law.

20. There shall be the right of all to own property either as individuals or as a member of a group.

21. There shall be the right to work for gain, within the philosophy of equal work for equal pay, and to establish businesses for gain, provided only always that in so doing public order is not disturbed and the rights of others are not infringed.

22. There shall be consultative mechanisms set up in which organised agriculture, mining, commerce, banking and industry participates to advise the Government on the best ways to avoid the dangers of free marketeering and exploitation on the one hand and the dangers of State control that curbs productivity on the other hand.

23. There shall be the right of all of protection by the State against unfair economic exploitation and it shall be the duty of the State to maximise and ensure the equitable distribution of wealth in the country.

The protection of minorities

24. There shall be protection of minorities in ways and means which do not violate the spirit of the statement and principles above and which do not violate the principles of democratic government in any way.

25. There shall be no domination of one group by any other group.

The politics of negotiation

26. WE NOW THEREFORE DECLARE that the above principles and statements can best be introduced to South Africa if a negotiated settlement is reached in non-violent debate and action and we declare our willingness to commence negotiations with the South African Government provided that negotiations initially deal only with meeting demands that:

26.1 All political prisoners be released from jail and a judicial body be established to act as an ombudsman to which political parties can appeal for the review of any particular case.

26.2 Legislation be enacted giving political parties the right to appeal to the courts to end a declared state of emergency when there are reasonable grounds to believe that in doing so normal law enforcement agencies can sufficiently protect life and property and keep good public order or appeal to the courts to prohibit any unnecessary use of troops in situations which would normally be a matter for the South African Police to deal with.

26.3 A mutually agreed procedure for the conduct of negotiations be devised by all negotiating parties.

26.4 After a successful conclusion of the negotiations a free and fair election for a new democratic Government for South Africa be held.

Negotiation as a process

27. In order to maximise the bridging of chasms that apartheid has created in South African society, due recognition must be given to the need to compromise. Black South Africans should reciprocate the boldness of the State President Mr F. W. de Klerk in politically stepping past lines of no returns by abandoning all-or-nothing politics.

28. Negotiation should strive to establish agreement on how best to achieve the salvation of the best that there is in South Africa while we jettison apartheid in part and in whole.

29. Nothing will be risked if, mindful of all those negotiating for the eradication of apartheid and the establishment of the kind of democracy spelt out above, the Government undertakes to enact legislation to give effect to decisions taken in the politics of negotiation as and when they are taken. The failure of the Government to do so would put opponents of apartheid nationally and internationally in a commanding political position.

Let there be trust in the Government's integrity until it is proven that trust must be withdrawn and let the South African Government trust that the opponents of apartheid will not destroy the politics of negotiation by combining forces to destroy the Government's image.

It is clear that the bitterness, the desire for revenge caused by apartheid and all its iniquities that I wrote about in earlier chapters, will not evaporate overnight. My long-held belief that there will be no post-apartheid Utopia also holds true. Certain apartheid legislation is still with us but it is clear that institutionalised racism can be negotiated out of existence.

I am encouraged by what the State President, Mr F. W. de Klerk, has done. I believe him to be sincere in his attempts to set South Africa, finally, on the road to democracy and to bring about the political equality of black and white. I have met Mr de Klerk four times in the past twelve months and during these meetings there was more real dialogue than there has been at all the meetings between myself and other former S.A. Heads of State put together.

As far as I am concerned South Africa's State President is earnest and shows all the signs of being competent to lead South Africa in the politics of change: to negotiate South Africa out of apartheid and to develop political models and a new constitution with the full involvement of black leaders which will leave the country with an open, race-free democracy.

What we are witnessing is more than a political act by a State President and a political party. We are seeing white society in transformation employing its inner resources to give expression to real moves forward into democracy.

It is agreed by all except the minority white extreme right-wing that apartheid is doomed and can never again rear its ugly head; it can and will be done away with. Consequently there is no need for blacks to fear bringing whites into the mainstream of democratic politics.

My views of Mr de Klerk's sincerity are shared by Dr Nelson Mandela and others inside South Africa, as well as by various leaders in Africa. There is also the precedent of the South African Government's dealings in Namibia which cannot be ignored when thinking about reform in this country.

The release of Dr Mandela and his prison colleagues and the unbanning of all the organisations including the ANC, PAC and the South African Communist Party and the de-restricting of persons and groups inside South Africa has, as I have outlined, given rise to a vast upsurge of political energy and fervour.

Institutionalised South Africa has been demanding the kind of moves Mr de Klerk is now making. This collective voice has been evident in black South Africa and organised mining, commerce, banking and industry, universities, churches and so on. They clearly support the reform process he has set in motion as numerous leaders in the West and in Africa have also done, specifically Mrs Margaret Thatcher, President George Bush, President Kenneth Kaunda, President Felix Houphouet-Boigny, President Daniel Arap Moi, His Majesty King Moshoeshoe II, President Mobutu and President Joaquim Chissano.

I return to my previous point however, in another way, that there are tragically far too many people in high places both in South Africa and in the United States, Great Britain, Europe, Australia, Canada and elsewhere, Africa included, who do not have vision enough to see that constructive support fuels the engine of change in South Africa.

To seek continued economic sanctions against South Africa and the continued international isolation of South Africa, as the ANC does, is now more tragically ill-conceived than ever before. To call for nationalisation, as the ANC continues to do, is just as ill-conceived.

I write this with a great deal of emphasis because that which is hanging in the balance in South Africa depends upon rapid change now being forthcoming which will be retarded by an international community that does not reward advances with relaxations in fields of disinvestment and other punitive actions against South Africa. Now is the time for investment, in all ways, in this country's future.

I base a lot of my thinking on the premise that mass spreading poverty is always destructive of democracy and I add to this basic perception that unless race groups are reconciled in South Africa we will not be able to develop the national will to produce the kind of wealth which could help governments of the future tackle backlogs in housing, education and social welfare facilities. Without being able to do so the unemployment and attending poverty that cannot be removed in the short term will breed the kind of discontent which has been totally destructive in places like Mozambique and Angola.

Political policies must be shaped to maximise the production of wealth and balances will have to be struck between some kind of marketeering free-enterprise system and the need for business and government to ward off threats of mass poverty.

I reject socialism, as I made clear in earlier chapters, out of hand and in tackling South Africa's land problems and poverty problems I do believe that there are alternatives to nationalisation, which Inkatha will table at the appropriate time. I make the point now that already Inkatha is seeking to clearly define future economic strategies, along with vital input from commerce, industry, academics and others, that will be constructive and have a hope of success. Soak-the-rich-to-feed-the-poor stances do not feature in our thinking.

Responsible balances can be struck between private enterprise and the need for State control in the same sort of patterns of West European social, democratic, thought. Free enterprise must be liberated simultaneously with the eradication of apartheid.

144

Free enterprise and government will have to get together to define their respective and joint responsibilities because both will have a vested interest in making sure that there is sufficient progress in improving the standards of living of the people to ensure that they continue to be willing to be governed as they are governed.

Free enterprise will become a major factor in the swinging balance of power during this crucial negotiating era which South African politics has entered. Like everything else in South Africa, there will have to be compromise on both sides of discussions between free enterprise and politics. Marxist or Socialist State control would be disastrous, but so would marketeering free enterprise clambering over the poor to grab what can be grabbed.

Times of transition are always risky and I ask all black and white leaders in South Africa and elsewhere to do everything in their power to minimise political risk for the country and not to risk South Africa's future for the sake of party political and ideological gain.

The road is now clear, to a very considerable extent, for black South Africa and white South Africa to meet each other half-way in an effort to get real talks and real negotiations on track. Compromises must be made provided that we are not expected to go as far as compromising the principles of democracy. We must be prepared to compromise in order to make negotiation possible.

My vision of a new South Africa being able to emerge in the not-too-distant future is possible and despite my great distress at the undemocratic and nihilistic behaviour being exhibited by some, I still have the utmost confidence and belief in the ordinary people of this country pulling together to build something great and lasting.

So now we have to look at how real negotiations can get on track. Can negotiations be held while there is still a State of Emergency in the country and violence continues? I call for the State of Emergency to be lifted. I also believe that citizens have a right to receive protection from the State. We are therefore, collectively, in a cleft-stick situation.

The ANC and Inkatha both want the State of Emergency to go. I'm sure the Government would like to do likewise but what then of the citizens who plead for State protection, who beg for safety they hope will be provided by the police and the Army to save their lives and their homes? People are under constant attack; entire families are being wiped out. That is the reality. Does the State sit back and wave an admonishing finger broadly telling youths and others who are literally killing machines to be good boys?

The State President has said, in my presence, that he wishes circumstances prevailed so that the State of Emergency could be lifted. He has added that the State of Emergency is 'not a political pawn' and should not be used to disrupt the political process. The regulations are in place to protect ordinary people.

Surely we must move on, no matter what, and recognise that it is institutionalised politics which will have to dominate centre-stage negotiations. Negotiations themselves must be negotiations between political parties and I argue that reform should now take on the nature of a process in which the Government legislates change into existence which is negotiated.

This process of legislating change, after step-by-step agreements lay the basis for common cause decisions, will play a vital role in defusing racial tensions, bridging racial chasms and eliminating bloodshed.

This approach will do more than any other to bring out the best that there is in South Africa and jettison the worst in ways which are acceptable to all. If this could be the theme of the politics of change, we will end up with a reconciled South Africa.

In a broad sense there already is common cause on the objectives of negotiation – to establish a non-racial, multi-party democracy in which there will be the rule of law, freedom of political association as well as all the great values expressed in the International Declaration of Human Rights.

Bitter differences, however, will emerge on questions about whether such ideals are achievable in a one-party democracy or better achievable in a multi-party democracy.

There is, however, perhaps not so much the chance of negotiations being bogged down at this level. If they falter it will more probably be because there are strong differences of opinion about how the process of negotiation should be managed and what form it should take.

As I have already outlined, the ANC has tabled its Harare document which asks for what amounts to the laying down of power by the South African Government and the handing over of power to some Namibia-type Constituent Assembly which will play midwife to a new constitution. I oppose such a move, as I have made clear. We need less racial tension, not more; we need less racial fears, not more. We do not need a scenario which will dramatically increase the strength of a white backlash. Some are acting now as if white South Africans don't count. I say they do count and should always count. I refuse to be a party to conducting future politics in South Africa in racist terms so that once negotiations have been concluded, they will be sidelined.

The State President, as I have said, has made irrevocable decisions to enter negotiations and there are no prospects whatsoever of apartheid being sustained. Blacks can therefore be ameliorative in the politics of negotiation and they can afford the give and take and the kind of compromises on central issues which will be needed to make progress.

This is why I say that blacks should negotiate for change in such a way that the South African Government just has to legislate changes into existence.

I am continually asked 'what of the future of homelands in a new South Africa?' This indicates a total lack of knowledge of where I have stood for all these years. I set up the Buthelezi Commission and was instrumental in the establishment of the KwaZulu-Natal Indaba and the KwaZulu-Natal Joint Executive Authority precisely because I have always seen KwaZulu and the Zulu nation as being part and parcel of a united South Africa.

I entered politics many decades ago because the Zulu nation – and black South Africa as a whole – was implacably opposed to all aspects of apartheid including the fragmentation of South Africa and the loss of our citizenship. Inkatha has become involved in pragmatic democratic action designed to eventually unite this country. All our efforts over the years have been structured to assist in the creation of a united non-racial South Africa.

Finally, I reaffirm my belief that the people of South Africa have the right to decide what the future of South Africa ought to be. They will decide the who's who of the first government after apartheid and they will decide who they want to pursue the formation of that first government. I struggle for the people's rights first and foremost.

Index

African National Congress (ANC) 7,
  8, 10; armed struggle 134; Harare
  Declaration 132-3, 138, 146; and
  Indaba 102; and Inkatha 104–5,
  131–2; and negotiated settlement
  98–100, 137, 138; sanctions 122, 144
Afrikanerdom 125-6
Albeldas, Michel 51–2
American Chamber of Commerce in
  SA 117
amnesty for exiles/refugees 91
Anglican Church, Lambeth
  conferences of 118
Anglo American Corporation 52–3
Angola 63
apartheid: and Afrikaner interests
  125–6; black fear of future 33; and
  capitalism 51–2; and churches 107;
  economically not viable 119, 124;
  eradication of, peaceful 77; final
  phase? 61–2, 69–71; international
  attitudes 17, 73–7, 110; internecine
  conflict 66, 79–80; in retreat 13, 16–
  17, 20, 48, 50, 55, 59, 60, 147;
  whites against 7–8, 126–7
Apprenticeship Act 62
arms embargo 124
Avis company 57

Badenhorst, Rev M. L. 117
Barclays Bank 124
bargaining power, black 48–9, 62, 124
Bhekuzulu ka Solomon, King Cyprian
  105
Bill of Rights, projected 25, 93–4, 95–
  6, 101
birthrate 38, 45

Black/White Joint Executive Authority
  (KwaZulu/Natal) 100
Boesak, Rev Allan 116
Boksburg 58
Botha, P. W. 48
Burnett, Archbishop Bill 106
Bush, President George 131, 143
Business Day (Johannesburg) 27, 30, 94

Camay, Phiroshaw 52
Cape Town 55, 56
capitalism see free enterprise system
Catholic Bishops' Conference (SA)
  117–18
Chissano, President Joaquim 143
Christian faith 9, 34, 106–14, 122–3,
  139; churches and sanctions 116-18
citizenship, right of 35, 80
civil war, threat of 76, 77–8
Coca Cola Company 124
Coetzee, Kobie 93
Colenso, Bishop John 106
Communism see Marxists/Leninists
Congress of South African Trade
  Unions 122
consensus 67–8, 84
Conservative Party 58, 60
constitutional reform 25, 33–6, 83, 94,
  95, 101; Inkatha Declaration 139–42;
  SA unique? 102, see also democracy
consumers, black 46, 54, 56, 57
Crossroads, Cape Town 56
Cuba 63

de Beer, Dr Zach 51
de Blank, Archbishop Joost 106

de Klerk, F. W. 46, 85, 88–9, 137; democratic process 142–3, 146, 147
de Soto, Hernando 40–2
Declaration of Intent 34–6
defence forces 26, 121, 133
democracy: ANC founders' aspirations 8, 10; de Klerk, dialogue with 142–3; National Party plan for form of? 87–8; survival of, in new SA 27–8, 30, 32, 80–2, *see also* constitutional reform
Dhloma, Dr Oscar 43, 79–80
diplomatic links 25
disease 47
disinvestment *see* sanctions
Durban 46, 56

earnings: comparisons, black/white 46
economy: future of 38–50; Inkatha views 63–4, 141; outside influences 125–7, *see also* free enterprise system; sanctions
education: expenditure 46, 144; fundamental importance 18–20, 26; higher 56, 78; Inkatha Declaration 140
employment 39
exile, factions in 10–11, 12–13, 14

First National Bank 124
Fischer, Alan 52
franchise, universal 33, 80, 85, 94, 96–7, 140
free-enterprise system: and democracy 64; must prove itself 25, 27–8, 30, 51–3; and State 144–5, *see also* economy; sanctions
freedom fighters 78, 110
Freeman, Charles 118

Gandhi, Mahatma 106
GNP in SA 44
Government *see* National Party Government
Group Areas Act 53, 55, 58, 88, 91, 92
'group rights' concept, Nationalist Government 86–7, 89, 91, 93, 95, 96
Guide, A, – South African Political Terms (Weichers) 101

Harare Declaration (ANC) 132–3, 138, 146
health services 26

homeland policies 103–4, 147
Houphouet-Boigny, President Felix 143
housing 37, 46, 57, 144
Hurley, Archbishop Denis 106
hygiene 47

IBM Company 124
illiteracy 37, 45
income distribution 57
Indaba (kwaZulu/Natal Indaba) 100–1
Influx Control regulations 16, 62
informal sector, the (of economy) 40–1
Inkatha 8, 20, 23, 36, 66, 68; and ANC 104–5, 131–2; 1990 Declaration 139–42; regional planning 100; role in new SA 81, 83, 84, 89, 147; Statement of Belief 63–4
International Chamber of Commerce (ICC) 115
international community: apartheid – double standards? 17, 71–3, 74–7; de Klerk initiatives 143–4; fictions about SA 44, 47; links with 25, *see also* Western democracies intimidation 15, 67, 69
investment capital needed: *see under* sanctions
Investor Responsibility Research Centre 118

Johannesburg 55, 57; diocesan view of Archbishop Tutu 116
John Paul II, Pope 82
journalism *see* press
judiciary 25, 85, 140

Kane-Berman, John 54, 58–9, 121
Kaunda, President Kenneth 61, 138, 143
Kennedy, Senator Edward 118
KwaZulu Government 20, 36, 68, 72, 81; against homeland policies 103–4; KwaZulu/Natal Indaba 100–1, 147; regional planning 100; report on impeded negotiations 90–3; role in new SA 84, 89

Law Commission (SA) report (1989) 93–7
leadership 24, 40, 113
Leatt, James 44
Lekota, Terror 131

liberation theology 106–14
liberty, definitions of 22-3
liquor consumption 57
local government as 'soft underbelly' of apartheid 54
Lutuli, Chief Albert 104, 106

management, need for black 46
Mandela, Dr Nelson 73, 90, 91, 99; after release 130, 135–6, 143; on participatory opposition 102–3
Marxists/Leninists 10, 41–2, 48, 145
Matthysen, Vernon 117
media treatment of SA politics 15, 30, 60–2
minority rights 85, 87, 96, 141
Mixed Marriages Act 17
Mobutu, President 143
Mogoba, Bishop Stanley 117
Moi, President Daniel Arap 143
mortality rates 47
Moshoeshoe II, King 143
Motsuenyane, Sam 117
Mozambique 39, 57
Mubarak, President Hosni 70–1

Namibia 143
Natal National Provincial Council 100
National Party Government 15–16; and constitution 62; divide and rule policies 68, 105; education targets 46; factions 60; future plans 30–1, 85–9, 137; homeland policy 103–4; joint report with KwaZulu on impeded negotiations 90–3; Law Commission report, and reform 93–8; need to negotiate with 31–2, 84–5; and 'silent revolution' 58–9; vulnerable 125–7
nationalisation 135, 144
Naude, Dr Beyers 106
negotiated settlement 83–100, 134–5, 137, 138, 142, 145–6
non-participation as strategy 102–3

Oliver, Mr Justice Pierre 93, 95
ombudsman 141
Operation Hunger 117
Organisation of African Unity (OAU) 70, 99, 132
Other Path, The: The Informal Revolution (de Soto) 40–1
Owen, Ken 27–8, 30, 94–5

pan-Africanism 26, 48; Pan African Congress (PAC) 98, 99
parliamentary systems 33, 34, 80–1, 85; tricameral 62, 87, 91, 92
Parsons, Raymond 38
Pass Laws 55–6, 62, 78
Paton, Dr Alan 122–3
Perlman, Ina 117
Peru, informal sector in 40–1
Pietersburg 57–8
police 26, 58, 133
population growth 37–8, 45
Population Registration Act 88, 91, 92
press: freedom of, in SA 92; and SA affairs 61–2
Pretoria/Witwatersrand/Vereeniging 46, 57
property ownership 27

Race Relations Survey (1987/8) 38
racism see apartheid
Ramaphosa, Cyril 51–2
reconciliation 8–9, 49, 68, 78, 136; ANC concerns 99
Relly, Gavin 53, 128–9
revolutionaries 7, 10–11, 12, 15–16; dangers from 39, 47, 70, 84; decisive action to counter 31; have no place in new SA 79; 'silent revolution', message of 55, see also violence
rule of law 26
S.A. Foundation Review 41
sanctions 115–28; alternatives to 128–9; black rejection 76–7; continued calls for 63, 135, 144; and GDP 46; investment capital needed 44–5, 127–8, 144; Western reasoning rejected 14, 42–3, 45, 110, see also economy; free enterprise system
sanitation 47
Savage, Bishop Thomas 106
schools 18–20
Schumpeter, J. A. 64–5
security forces 26, 121, 133
self-determination, principle of 87
Separate Amenities Act 16, 91, 92
'silent revolution' 54–9, 78
Simelane, Rev. S. D. 106
social welfare 25, 144
socialism 28–9, 51, 144, 145; failures of 64–5; Mozambique 39; one-party state 69–70

South African Council of Churches 122

South African Institute of Race Relations (SAIRR) 46, 54, 55, 121

Southern Africa Black Taxi Association (SABTA) 57

Soviet Union 39, 63; and ANC 99

Soweto 57

State of Emergency 15, 92, 145–6

strikes 54

Struggle Has Many Tactics, The (Mandela) 102–3

suffrage, universal 33, 80, 85, 94, 96–7, 140

Sunday Times 74

Suzman, Helen 43, 118

Tambo, Oliver 73, 104

taxis, black 57–8

teacher training colleges 56

technikons 56

terrorism 11–12

Thatcher, Margaret 77, 131, 143

trade unions 25, 54, 121, 140; black rights 58, 60–1

tricameral parliamentary system 62, 87, 91, 92

Tutu, Archbishop Desmond 51, 116, 138

Ubunto-Botho, ideal of 8, 9

Umkhonto we Sizwe 99

unemployment 37, 40, 44, 119–20, 133–4

United Democratic Front 122, 131

United Nations 14, 132

United States of America 63

Universal Declaration of Human Rights 122, 146

universities 26, 56

urbanisation 56

van Wyk, Chris 120

violence: ANC's changing attitudes 7, 8, 10; internecine 66–7, 69, 73, 133; no way forward 13, 34, 36, 63, 78, 110; terrorism 11–12, *see also* revolutionaries

Vlok, Adriaan 59

Washington Post 43

wealth, creation of *see* economy

Weichrs, Professor Marinus 101

Western democracies: and freedom fighters 78, 110; pressure for negotiation 99, 133; sanctions 42–3, 45, 76–7, 115, 118, 123–4, 127–8; views of post-apartheid SA 47, *see also* international community

white South Africans: against apartheid 7–8; fear of future 28–9, 30, 32–3, 36, 137, 138–9; sanctions 121, 125; seeking democratic change 94, 105, 143; terrorism, right-wing 11, 77

Wiehan Commission 61

Xaba, Canon 106

Zulu, Bishop Alphaeus 106